Performatively Speaking

Performatively Speaking

Speech and Action in Antebellum American Literature

Debra J. Rosenthal

University of Virginia Press

Charlottesville & London

University of Virginia Press
© 2015 by the Rector and Visitors of the University of Virginia
All rights reserved
Printed in the United States of America
on acid-free paper

First published 2015

1 3 5 7 9 8 6 4 2

Library of Congress Cataloging-in-Publication Data
Rosenthal, Debra J., 1964–
  Performatively speaking : speech and action in antebellum
American literature / Debra J. Rosenthal.
    pages   cm
  Includes bibliographical references and index.
  ISBN 978-0-8139-3696-3 (cloth : acid-free paper) — ISBN 978-
0-8139-3697-0 (pbk. : acid-free paper) — ISBN 978-0-8139-3698-7
(e-book)
  1. American fiction—19th century—History and criticism. 2.
Speech in literature. I. Title.
  PS374.S735R67 2015
  813'.309—dc23

2014025631

Contents

Acknowledgments

I am indebted to various scholars who helped push me to think more deeply about my ideas. I owe a huge thanks to Michael J. Davey, Faye Halpern, Cindy Hamilton, Steven Hayward, Barbara Hochman, Katie Horowitz, Denise Kohn, David LaGuardia, Brian Macaskill, John McBratney, Jon Miller, Bob Nowatzki, Wesley Raabe, Sarah Robbins, Katherine Kish Sklar, and Joyce Warren for reading various chapters and offering valuable feedback. I smile with warmth and gratitude when I think of fellow intellectual adventurer Joanne Friedman. Her readerly insights and ability to hone in on a literary argument are unmatched. Nancy Armstrong's brilliance accomplished in ten minutes what would have taken me months; I am thankful for her acumen. It was my great fortune to meet and befriend Agnieszka Soltysik Monnet at the Université de Lausanne, who created opportunities for me to present my work at Swiss conferences, meet fellow scholars, and lecture in her classroom at UNIL. Although it has been a long time since I was a graduate student in their classrooms at Princeton University, I owe my growth as a scholar to Lee Clark Mitchell, Maria DiBattista, and A. Walton Litz, my original teachers.

The many meetings of the Northeast Nineteenth-Century American Women Writers study group over the past fifteen years have proven so valuable for providing intellectual support and cultivating research topics. In particular, the ideas for this book's chapter on promises evolved from the meeting on gift books held at Rutgers University in the spring of 2012.

Several faculty summer research fellowships from John Carroll University allowed me to complete individual chapters. Most of all, the university was extremely generous in awarding me a Grauel Faculty Fellowship for a year's sabbatical to finish writing this book. The wonderful insights and support of David S. Reynolds were instrumental in helping me secure the funding. I am extremely grateful for my university's support.

Many thanks to Nevin Mayer, Adam Green, and Brandon Walker at John Carroll University's Grasselli Library and to graduate students Rachel Hoag and Ann Visintainer for their research savvy in tracking down articles while I was overseas. As always, I am grateful to Norma B. Piccirillo and James Burrows for professionally handling my manuscript.

I am grateful to the anonymous readers for the University of Virginia Press, whose suggestions for revisions were very astute. I am indebted to my editor, Cathie Brettschneider, for being so supportive of this project and for her keen insights. I greatly appreciate Morgan Myers's astute suggestions and detailed attention to my manuscript.

When a certain someone (whom I will not name lest I feel an urge to throttle him) erased my book and all backup copies, the formidable forensic skills of Mark Johnson saved me and earned my eternal admiration and gratitude.

The quiet solitary days of writing were brightened by two sweet fuzzy faces whose meows for attention kept me happy company.

Christie Gascoigne's exuberant example of how to be present keeps me breathing, stretching, and full of joy. Namaste.

Although perhaps only detectable on the page by me right now, the sustaining energy of many friends imbues every word I've written. I wish I could acknowledge them all, but must especially mention the enduring, supportive friendship of Jill Bieler, Miriam Friedman, Cindy Gherman, Shari Goldberg, Anna Hocevar, Jeanne Longmuir, Susan Piszel, Wendy Sattin, Maria Sonaro, and Rachel Weiss.

While I was living overseas as I brought this book to completion, several new friends played a critical role in creating a supportive atmosphere for me in which to work productively. I treasure the friendship, confidence, easy laugh, and keen interpersonal insights of Janet Waring, my friend, neighbor, and walking partner; I dearly miss her company and our full-hearted conversations. My Monday morning walking group of smart, fun-loving, and encouraging women kept me sane during the difficult final push to finish: Karen Brace, Anna Fabri-Colovan, Chris Linford, and Isabelle Vernet. Larry Rosenthal's almost-daily overseas calls as he walked to work in the mornings nurtured me with a welcome afternoon respite from writing, and I am grateful for Brenda, Rebecca, and Nicole Comisar's overseas visit that brought a bit of home to our corner of the French/Swiss border.

My mom, Joan Seldin Rosenthal, is always a shining homing beacon, pointing me towards what is good and true. My dad, Marvin J. Rosenthal, the consummate collector of ideas and people, would have been so pleased with this book. I wish he had lived long enough to kvell over it.

Ultimately, everything points to the three people who constitute my whole world: my husband, Glenn Starkman, and my children, Nathaniel and Ariana. With unflagging interest and constant and loving encouragement, they have theorized performativity with me, shared Hester Prynne's trials with me, fumed with me about Tom and slavery, accompanied me onboard the *Pequod* to hunt for the whale, listened to enough about temperance literature to drive them to drink, and always made me feel the value of my work. It was very gratifying to be all together working side by side in our living room on the night I finished writing this book. Since they have by now absorbed enough theory to be experts in the performativity of language, I hereby declare that this book is dedicated to them.

Performatively Speaking

Discursive Action, or Doing by Saying

In T. S. Arthur's 1854 novel *Ten Nights in a Bar-Room and What I Saw There,* Joe Morgan grieves for his young daughter Mary who lies in bed dying from a head wound received at the Sickle and Sheaf tavern. Mary had gone to the tavern to drag home her drunken father but was accidently hit in the head with a drinking glass thrown by the tavern owner, who was aiming for Joe. From her sick bed, Mary pleads with her father not to go out at night until her health recovers: "Do promise just that, father, dear" (64).

In this highly sentimental scene, Joe cannot resist his daughter's loving insistence, and despite his longing for a drink, he capitulates with, "I promise it, Mary; so shut your eyes now and go to sleep" (ibid.). Mary then tells her father, "You feel better for that promise; I know you do." Joe reluctantly concedes to himself that uttering the promise has effected a change in his spirit: "He does feel better but is hardly willing to admit it" (ibid.). Joe wants to promise that he will never drink at the Sickle and Sheaf ever again, but he cannot bring himself to say something with such long-term effects: his "resolution just lacks the force of utterance" (63).

By uttering "I promise it," Joe creates an agreement between himself and his daughter; he obliges himself to be housebound and thus brings a measure of relief to the dying Mary. Assurances such as Joe's ameliorate a desperate family situation and point toward a bright prospect of sobriety and respectability. Promises can be viewed as social rituals that bind or connect; emotionally and psychically, however, promises can constitute so much more, especially as Joe's promise restores Mary's faith in him. While a broken business contract incurs financial penalties, a broken personal promise can lead to heartbreak. Were Joe to break his vow and start drinking again, Mary would be devastated not just by the fact of his inebriation, but by the failure of Joe's words to bind him to his intention.

I

When Joe makes his promise not to drink, he uses language differently than he would to discuss his desire to patronize the tavern. When Joe promises, he does not merely remark about the fact that he intends not to drink in the future; likewise, Mary does not hear a man discussing the benefits of temperance. Rather, Joe uses what is known as a performative: when he utters "I promise," he engages in the act of promising. The act of stating *I promise* is to actually promise; it stands as the reference of the utterance. As performative speech, a promise brings a situation or event of promising into existence by virtue of its being uttered. Promising enacts its very purport; uttering a promise redoubles as an action. Joe Morgan's "I promise" inaugurates a different condition than a mere statement of fact.

Performatively Speaking: Speech and Action in Antebellum American Literature examines mid-nineteenth-century American writers' concerns with the potential for language not just to represent action, but to be action in and of itself. That is, the book investigates moments where authors no longer distinguish between writing and doing but instead explore what happens when words act. In examining antebellum literary texts, particularly those written during the half-decade of 1850-55, also known as the American Renaissance, this book addresses the ways writers understood what critics today, over a century later, now call performative speech theory or speech-act theory. Performative speech can be described as an utterance that creates or produces the very action it names. A performative differs from a constative—the way we normally use language to describe something or to convey ideas—because a performative summons an action into existence by virtue of stating it and thus creates the social reality it expresses. Naming thereby doubles as enacting; speech reveals itself to be action.

In addition to the act of promising, another example many critics give of a performative utterance is an officiant at a wedding who intones, "I now pronounce you husband and wife." Such an officiant does not report that a wedding occurred but actually instantiates the marriage through words. The officiant's utterance has force and legal standing; the couple will be married only as the officiant enacts the marriage through the performative utterance.[1] Because of the performative power of the officiant's words, only a lawyer and untold thousands of dollars can undo the marriage. The 2012 action movie *The Expendables 2* plays on the potency of such an utterance: in order to ambush his enemies, Jason Statham's character, Lee Christmas, dresses as a priest. He launches a surprise attack while wearing the religious robes and solemnly intones, "By the power vested in me, I now pronounce you man and knife." He then stabs and kills all the bad guys in sight. Viewers might debate which is more painful—the stabbings or the corny line. Despite its dubious humor, the line illustrates some elements of performativity: the word *pronounce* creates the condition of pronouncing; as a trained special forces soldier, Lee Christmas does indeed have the power to kill vested in him; and the "man and knife" pun does emphasize that Lee Christmas intimately and powerfully unites the enemies with their death via a deadly knife.

The performative *I pronounce* is not the same as the words *I see* or *I walk* because it enacts the very idea it states. *I see* is not the same thing as seeing; *I walk* is not the act of walking. John Searle illustrates the concept by writing, "I can't fix the roof by saying, 'I fix the roof' and I can't fry an egg by saying, 'I fry an egg,' but I can promise to come and see you just by saying, 'I promise to come and see you'" ("How Performatives Work" 535). "I pronounce" therefore discursively enacts its very purport and creates a new situation (a legally binding marriage) where none could exist without the utterance. The officiant's words do not describe an existing state of affairs in the real world but rather, according to Richard van Oort, bring "a state of affairs *into existence* by virtue of [an] utterance. The act of naming is *simultaneously* the reference of [the] statement. The performative is therefore, in the most rigorous sense, an *act* and not a representation of something else, at least not in the preferred constative sense of a representation" (n.p.). Accordingly, *Performatively Speaking* examines how mid-nineteenth-century American writers wrestled with the ways language could be so powerful that it could constitute action; in other words, the book examines the ways words can lead to, or can themselves be, actions with physical (and sometimes violent) results. To elucidate the discourse–deed connection, this book investigates the self-binding nature of the promise, the formulaic but transformative temperance pledge, the power of Ruth Hall's signature or name on legal documents, the punitive hate speech of Hester Prynne's scarlet letter *A*, the prohibitionary voodoo hex of Simon Legree's slave Cassy, and Captain Ahab's injurious insults to his second mate Stubb.

The most formidable thinker about speech acts, J. L. Austin, originally shared his ideas in an initially poorly received series of twelve lectures delivered for Harvard's William James Lectures series in 1955. By the last lecture, only a few stragglers attended. Both Jacques Derrida and Paul de

Man were at Harvard at the time of Austin's lectures, but neither attended the series. According to de Man, "The word around Harvard was that a somewhat odd and quirky Oxford don was giving a series of rather dull and inscrutable lectures" (quoted in Miller 61).

Austin's lectures were published posthumously in 1962 as the influential *How to Do Things with Words*. In the lecture series and book, Austin carefully explains that the right conditions must exist in order for a performative to work correctly. He specifies that "there must exist an accepted conventional procedure having a certain conventional effect, that procedure to include the uttering of certain words by certain persons in certain circumstances" (14). That is, the right words must be said by the right people in the right situation. If in class one day I were to tell my students, "I hereby pronounce you graduates of John Carroll University," they would be puzzled because I do not hold the requisite authority to utter such words meaningfully. Only on graduation day will those words, when uttered by the university president, turn my students into potential donors to be targeted by development officers for endowment gifts. A successfully executed performative Austin terms "felicitous" or "happy." Unless uttered under the right conditions, a performative will fail; Austin terms such a failure an infelicitous utterance or a misfire, misapplication, misexecution, or misinvocation (17).[2]

Austin distinguishes among several types of speech acts. He terms a "locutionary act" any "equivalent to uttering a certain sentence with a certain sense and reference" (109). Most communication would fall under this category of using words to convey an idea. Austin calls "perlocutionary" those utterances that bring about action. For example, if one of my children were to say, "I'm hungry," I would prepare him or her a snack; the statement of hunger describes a condition and causes me to act. However, *Performatively Speaking* principally concerns what Austin terms an "illocutionary" utterance, where the action described is performed by the utterance itself—or, as Eve Kosofsky Sedgwick quips, "illocution is where the action is" (78). Austin admits that "it is the distinction between illocutions and perlocutions which seems likeliest to give trouble" (110), and he goes on at great length distinguishing between the two.[3] As an example of the trickiness of determining the difference, Austin argues that the phrase *I warn you that* constitutes an illocutionary utterance but *I convince you that* does not (131). And even though the term *speech act* refers to a wide variety of linguistic phenomena, the term often refers specifically to an illocutionary act.

Austin complicates the idea of the performative by distinguishing between what he terms explicit and implicit performatives. Most successful performatives have a verb in the first-person singular present active indicative (ibid. 67). Explicit performatives "begin with or include some highly significant and unambiguous expression such as 'I bet,' 'I promise,' 'I bequeath'—an expression very commonly also used in naming the act which, in making such an utterance, I am performing—for example betting, promising, bequeathing" (32). As an example of an implicit performative, Austin cites the utterance "go," because by saying it one can "achieve practically the same as we achieve by the utterance 'I order you to go'" (ibid.). By introducing the idea of an implicit performative that is "practically the same" as an explicit one, Austin leaves open and flexible the decidability and fixedness of such speech acts. He writes that it "is left uncertain when we use so inexplicit a formula as the mere imperative 'go,' whether the utterer is ordering (or is purporting to order) me to go or merely advising, entreating, or what not me to go. . . . In a given situation it can be open to me to take it as *either* one or the other" (32–33).

This confusion about implicit or explicit ramifies to a larger question of whether an utterance is performative or constative. For example, "I assert that this distinction is confusing" is both performative, since one felicitously asserts by the act of saying "I assert," and simultaneously constative because it states a fact about the distinction. Reading *How to Do Things with Words* can convince anyone that an utterance's performativity might be difficult, if not impossible, to pin down. One category melds into another, leading J. Hillis Miller to ask, "What use are these distinctions if they do not really serve to distinguish?" (17). While Austin outlines how performatives might differ from constative statements, John Searle's essay "How Performatives Work" tries to reconcile detractors who claim that all performatives are indeed statements of one order. *Performatively Speaking* investigates moments where mid-nineteenth-century authors understand this possible distinction and play with the action potential of words.

The weakest part of Austin's theory comes when he discusses speech act theory in terms of creative writing or the literary imagination. Austin dismisses the speech acts of a poet or an actor on the stage by downgrading such speech to the rank of "parasitic" or "peculiar" or not "ordinary."

According to Austin, a performative is "hollow or void" if occurring in a poem or spoken in a soliloquy. He thus excludes fictional or imaginative speech from any consideration of meaning for the performative (22). From that point of view, my project in *Performatively Speaking* would be irrelevant because, in Austinian terms, fictional characters' words stand as hollow and void since penned by an author and not uttered in a "real" situation. I disagree with Austin and instead want to redirect focus to the ways antebellum authors understood the inherent performativity of language. By placing discursively active words in their characters' mouths or pens (or, in Hester Prynne's case, her needle), the authors included in this book create and substantiate linguistic situations and actions. They thus prove themselves to be nascent practitioners of performativity before such a theory was codified.

Austin describes the performative as an utterance that is neither "true" nor "false" but "in which to say something is to do something, or in saying something we do something, or even *by* saying something we do something" (109). With his codification of the ways "saying makes it so," Austin's work has generated many, many responses. While Austin seems to fear that language would be "infected" (21) or contaminated by taking seriously the performative nature of literature, Jacques Derrida, for example, asserts that this very contamination underwrites language's performativity. Derrida argues that Austin erroneously casts such linguistic "impurity" as "the place of external perdition which speech could never hope to leave" (*Limited Inc,* 17).[4] Derrida also distinguishes between citation and iteration: a citation repeats or mimics words and their original context, whereas an iteration "alters, something new takes place" (ibid. 40). Since according to Austin a felicitous performative must be composed of the right words in the right situation, the right words by definition must be a citation; the performative works by repeating known combinations of words.

Yet a performative can likewise be achieved via iteration: novelists create new and vibrant contexts in which their words perform. Derrida asks, "Could a performative succeed if its formulation did not repeat a 'coded' or iterable utterance, or in other words, if the formula that I pronounce in order to open a meeting, launch a ship or a marriage were not identifiable as *conforming* with an iterable model, if it were not then identifiable in some way as a 'citation'?" (ibid. 18). Miller summarizes the difference by saying that "citation is supposed to drag its original context implicitly along with it, while iteration may use the same words in a radically new context" (71).[5] To Derrida, such a clear distinction is not always possible: "a paradoxical but unavoidable conclusion" is that "a successful performative is necessarily an 'impure' performative" (*Limited Inc* 17).

However, as I will discuss in the second chapter, Derrida makes a complicated argument that at times the performative creates its own context in which to be effective. Thus, I want to argue that performative speech occurring in fiction, while perhaps more iterative than citational (if one cleaves to such distinctions) because of the new contexts and characters in novelists' imaginative worlds, is not hollow, void, parasitic, or etiolated (all Austin's words). In agreeing with Derrida that "impure" fictional utterances stand as just as relevant as words spoken by "real" people, I find it critically important to subject antebellum American literature to theories of performativity.

Far from ossified, Austin's ideas have a renewed energy as they have been taken up by literary and cultural theory, performative studies, philosophy, and theories of sexuality and gender. By reading antebellum American literature with an eye towards performativity, we can invigorate our understanding of speech acts by flexing and complicating the way such critical reading practices intersect with mid-nineteenth-century texts. As several critics have noted, a topic of debate in mid-nineteenth-century America was how language might reflect physical, spiritual, and moral truths.[6] For example, Elizabeth Varon wrote an entire study about the power of the word *disunion* in the antebellum period. She argues that "debates over the meaning of disunion constituted a rhetorical mode that dominated antebellum politics and that gave sectional tensions an unmanageable cast. That is, disunion rhetoric shaped and limited Americans' political and moral imagination, ultimately discouraging a politics of compromise and lending an aura of inexorability to the cataclysmic confrontation of North and South" (2). To Varon, the word *disunion* had the performative effect of serving (in the words of her section subtitles) as prophecy, threat, accusation, process, and program. The word *disunion* created and substantiated situations that were formative and influential in the antebellum period. Both of our studies draw upon scholars who theorize language's capacity to conjure and shape political reality.

The 1850s seemed to be a period characterized by more doubt about the status of language than the 1840s, which was a decade full of heady and earnest public speeches, young men's lyceum circuits, heated temperance activism, religious revival, the confidence placed by the transcendental-ists in seeing the unity of all things through the way language connects the spirit to nature, and the success of the Second Great Awakening. The discourse in the 1850s turned from moral suasion towards more political activism, as confidence in the power of words to persuade seemed to fade in favor of the need for more efficacious legislation in the years leading up to the Civil War. The writers that I study in this book demonstrate that words can indeed restructure power, but not through gentle principled suasion. In a time period of fervent moral reform and social legislation, these writers show that action-oriented discourse is more relevant and essential to a changing society.

Speech act theory can help develop a fuller critical account of linguistic and discursive action in the antebellum period, particularly since much current criticism about the period focuses on sentimentalism and evoca-tion of feeling. Feeling comprises an important part of interpreting, and scholars rightfully address how feeling leads to action (weeping, spine-tingling chills, laughing, anger, etc.), but I focus on moments when a feeling or idea functions as action.

For a long time critics believed that popular mid-nineteenth-century women novelists were sole regents of the empire of sentimental discourse, a discourse that was meant to evoke strong emotions in the reader. But since the publication of a special issue of *American Literature* entitled "No More Separate Spheres" and Mary Chapman and Glenn Hendler's *Senti-mental Men*, critics have overturned the long-in-vogue "separate spheres" paradigm. Moreover, scholars of American literature have moved past the critical moment that redeemed the "scribbling women writers" from critical neglect. My inquiry into discursive action borrows heavily from studies about sentimentalism and domesticity, but reads relevant literary moments as acts, not feelings. The question of gender is not at the fore-front of my study but emerges as a major concern for Harriet Beecher Stowe and Fanny Fern, for whom the volatility of speech risked being interpreted as anti-feminine and thus threatening.

Performatively Speaking coincides with a growing interest in affect stud-ies, which explores the emotional effects of literary texts on readers.[7] For example, books like Michael Millner's *Fever Reading,* Eve Kosofsky Sedg-wick's *Touching Feeling,* and Jane Thrailkill's *Affecting Fiction* study emo-tion and nineteenth-century American literature from multi-genre and interdisciplinary perspectives. But rather than focusing on such sentimental effects—and how such effects were theorized by nineteenth-century authors themselves—*Performatively Speaking* pushes the critical dialogue to inquire how such effects arise from the action inherent in the act of uttering. Millner acknowledges that words can lead to action: "Reading badly means reading that causes you to lose a sense of self or free will, reading that is addictive, reading that makes you chronically distracted or, alternatively, reading that completely absorbs you" (xiii). These types of reading are considered "delinquent and pathological" because they "dissolve critical distance and undercut the possibility of reflection—elements thought essential to a proper public sphere and good citizenship" (ibid. xiii). *Performatively Speaking* complement William Reddy's work on emotives, which he discusses as being a "departure" from speech-act theory. Reddy writes that "when one makes an emotion claim in the presence of another, one hears the words, one sees the other's reception of the claim, one feels one's face contracting in suggestive ways. Emotives can thus be used as tools for arriving at desired states. . . . Rather than confirming the state described, they may produce the opposite effect or no effect" (322). My study does not deny that words lead to action, but it complements affect studies by tangentially providing an analysis of what happens when words themselves serve as action.

Writers and intellectuals debated theories of language for centuries before Austin codified his ideas of performative speech. Ralph Waldo Emerson stood as the reigning man of letters of the early nineteenth century who most directly influenced the authors discussed in *Performatively Speaking*. While it is beyond the purview of my book to engage with Emerson's ideas at length, I do want to highlight some of his thoughts that perhaps most immediately affected his contemporaries. In his essay "Eloquence," Emerson discussed the influence and clout of oratory in the period. Emerson believed that a speaker's word could not be separated from action: "It is the electricity of action. It is action, as the general's word of command or chart of battle is action" (61). The authors discussed in *Performatively Speaking* demonstrate the application of Emerson's dictum: their works posit the ways that discursivity and deed coalesce as one.

In the "Language" section of "Nature," perhaps Emerson's most direct and elaborate working out of ideas about language, he famously writes, "Words are signs of natural facts." In this belief in the close association between words and nature—that words are signs that emerge from humans' relationship to the natural world—Emerson advocates a mimetic view of language. He sees human language as less indebted to society than to the native environment (Garvey 23). The authors I discuss share an understanding of language's ability to embody action that resonates with Emerson's theories. They see language as the "electricity of action" that contains the ability to merge the symbolism of words with natural unmediated action.

Finally, as a preacher, Emerson derived from the long rich tradition that understood the pulpit to be the source of exhortation, moral reform, and action. The figure of the minister used the powerful action potential of words to ignite awe, reverence, fear, and devotion in parishioners. Emerson's hortatory essays share much in common with the sermonic language of *Uncle Tom's Cabin*, the celebratory fervor of pledge-makers in temperance tales, and the preaching of the various sermons in *Moby-Dick*. Emerson's essays and preaching demonstrated that writers could harness the transformative potential of words, a power similarly understood by the writers examined in *Performatively Speaking*.

Although philosophers, anthropologists, linguists, legal theorists, computer scientists, and psychologists also talk about speech acts, *Performatively Speaking* differs from any work in those disciplines by the way it is thoroughly rooted in close textual literary analysis. *Performatively Speaking* ranges widely through mid-nineteenth-century culture and touches on many subfields within American literary studies, such as disability studies, alcohol studies, sentimentalism and theories of sympathy and empathy, feminist literary studies, and rhetorical studies.[8] Although the book is deeply indebted to Judith Butler's ideas of injurious language, hate speech, and the subversive potential of speech acts, my inquiry into the intersection of language and action does not emphasize the construction of identity, leftwing cultural politics, the unity of the liberal subject, legal discourse, or minority rights.

In applying some aspects of speech act theory to literary works, I aim to head in a new direction. By using theories of the performativity of language to examine nineteenth-century fiction, *Performatively Speaking* opens up discussion about the role of discursive action in texts both canonical and noncanonical. Performative speech embodies the close link between words and action and can thus help the reader overcome constraints of descriptive representation. With its unmediated access to the reader, discursive action helps readers engage deeply with the text. My selection of such major texts as *The Scarlet Letter, Uncle Tom's Cabin,* and

Moby-Dick anchors the book in mid-century literature; my choice to read those texts alongside Fanny Fern's *Ruth Hall* and temperance fiction and essays shows the relevance of considering the ramifications of speech as action in a wider selection of antebellum literature.

The opening chapter, "Slave Promises and the Temperance Pledge," explores selected moments of extrajudicial promises to investigate the way some mid-nineteenth-century American writers theorized the force of the act of voluntary verbal self-binding. A particularly interesting type of promise that we find in antebellum American literature, one that conflates issues of bondage and self-binding, is the slave's voluntary promise to his or her master. The act of promising sets up a curious condition for one legally held in bondage. The U.S. judicial system upheld slavery by the force of signatures on legal bills of sale, but the slaves themselves could only be objects of exchange within contracts, never the signing subject. Thus, I am very curious about what happens when a slave voluntarily inaugurates herself or himself in the continued process of bondage by performatively engaging in the act of promising.

The chapter also examines the effects of self-binding that result from the performative act of signing or stating the temperance pledge. While promising or pledging entails self-restraining, the temperance pledge liberated because it freed the drunkard from the chains of inebriation. The chapter explores the performativity of the utterances that bring about such monumental action and change in the inebriated. In scene after scene in nineteenth-century temperance fiction, drunken men, particularly fathers, sign an oath of abstinence in an overdetermined mawkish moment meant to be the highpoint of the story. At the conversion moment when the men pledge to be sober, women characters sob, readers rejoice, and author, reader, and characters all join together in mutual understanding and redemption. Such scenes draw heavily from sentimental convention; indeed, the success of a temperance tale depended on its ability to elicit a deep emotional and sympathetic response from the reader. At the same time, the promissory utterance transforms the speaking subject into one beholden to his or her own words. The chapter examines temperance fiction to demonstrate how the temperance vow oscillates between sentimental feeling and performative action and questions what it means for a speech act to be a speech feeling and how the efficacy of sentiment is indebted to its performativity.

While the opening chapter teases out the ways that interpersonal promises can bind as surely, if not more strongly, than standard legal contracts, the second chapter pushes the investigation of performativity to the idea of the signature. Signed documents enact a promise that validates and legitimates legal agreements. "Theorizing the Signature in Fanny Fern's *Ruth Hall*" discusses how the heroine of Fern's important 1854 novel needs to sign legal contracts with her publisher in order to guarantee her payment and to clarify her obligation to the newspapers. I examine Fern's novel with an eye towards understanding the performativity of Ruth's signature, the presence of which indicates the absence of the signer.

The signature enacts an identity, and one that can be problematic for a single woman being ushered into the public space of the market and publishing. *Ruth Hall* is greatly concerned with the ways Ruth enters into the business world as a marketable commodity herself, whereby Ruth uttering her name and pseudonym performs an action and enacts identity as well as litigable powers. I am particularly interested in Fern's curious choice to reproduce the image of a bank stock at the end of the novel—the only image in the book. By showing readers the stock note and its legal language ("Be it known that Mrs. Ruth Hall," etc.), Fern transforms Ruth's identity from pauper to stockholder. The stock can be said to utter Ruth's name in such a way as to constitute an action that rearranges Ruth's relationship to capital and the market. Furthermore, Ruth's choice to sign her writings using the pseudonym "Floy" raises many previously unconsidered questions about the utterance of a name in relation to the novel's politics, authenticity, and the gendered nature of the iterability of her signature. This chapter intervenes in studies of Fern and the rise of the woman writer by focusing on the gendered nature of the signature and the ways a woman's absence signifies presence by means of writing her name.

After theorizing the writing of the signature, the book turns in the third chapter to the figure of a single alphabetical character: the embroidered letter Hester Prynne wears on her dress. "The Scarlet *A* as Action" builds a theory of Nathaniel Hawthorne's scarlet letter *A* itself. In *The Scarlet Letter* Hawthorne writes that Puritan society views Hester Prynne and her scarlet letter as "a living sermon" and "the text of the discourse"; I am interested in how exactly Hester's scarlet badge articulates such a sermon or text. If the scarlet *A* is speech, what does it say? If it is an act, what does it do? If we subject Hester's scarlet utterances ("a living sermon" and "the text of the discourse") to the pressures of performative speech theory, then rather than seeing the letter *A* as a statement or comment about Hester's moral or spiritual situation we can investigate many questions about the performativity of language in Hawthorne's novel and how to do things with a letter. Considering the scarlet letter as a speech act helps readers see that the letter *A* constitutes an action with injurious results, not just a moral evaluation of Hester.

I am interested in the way that the scarlet *A*, as performative speech, both adheres to and resists convention and thereby variously affects Hester and her fellow townspeople. The chapter uses arguments about pornographic speech and hate speech to show that the *A* can simultaneously utter both the injurious litigious language of the Puritans and Hester's performative dissent. The chapter also examines other ways the scarlet letter acts, especially since it functions as sexualized speech. I look at the way that Pearl's green seaweed *A* and Dimmesdale's deathbed self-flagellation fail as speech acts. Ultimately, the chapter argues that Hester's embroidery of the scarlet *A* co-opts the magistrates' official speech, reclaims the injurious language, cites it, and reassigns its authority. I read the scarlet letter as performative speech to show that Hawthorne stages a theory of the performativity of language, in language itself, at the level of the most basic utterance—a single letter.

Whereas Hester's utterance of the scarlet letter produces much ambiguity, the threatening utterance of the slave Cassy in Harriet Beecher Stowe's *Uncle Tom's Cabin* seems quite clear to her overseer. The fourth chapter, "Verbal Violence in *Uncle Tom's Cabin*," proposes a new reading of an important but neglected scene in chapter 33, in which Cassy defiantly challenges Sambo as he threatens to whip her for assisting Tom. The scene replicates an iconic moment: the angry slave driver stands with an upraised whip over the crouching slave. But instead of cowering in fear, Cassy threatens to "say the word" if Sambo whips her; Sambo fearfully lowers his whip. For years I had wondered about this scene: what could a defenseless slave say to an overseer with a whip? Finally I came up with an answer by reading the scene through the lens of performative speech theory in order to raise questions about the mutually constitutive nature of language and action that is so central to Stowe's strategy of sympathetic identification through domestic sentimentality. I read Cassy's retort in light of pan-African vodun and the rich syncretic milieu of mid-nineteenth-century New Orleans. I suggest that understanding Cassy's speech as performative forces us to rethink Stowe's use of suasive techniques and the links between sentiment and action.

Although Cassy does not need to level verbal violence against Sambo, Captain Ahab does produce injury with his words. The book's final chapter, "Action and Injurious Speech in *Moby-Dick*," opens with the moment in Herman Melville's novel in which Captain Ahab roars at his second mate, Stubb, "Down, dog, and kennel!" Stubb feels so hurt and wounded by this insult that he questions whether Ahab injured him verbally or corporeally. He is not sure whether Ahab actually kicked him or merely hurled an oral rebuke. Ahab's insult here is thought by Stubb to be an action that has a performative effect—it carries a force within it and constitutes Stubb as an injured party. If Ahab's words can be seen as having an injurious effect tantamount to a physical kick, then what is the status of words if Stubb is uncertain how to interpret the language? Stubb also wonders whether a kick by Ahab should be less harmful since Ahab's leg is a prosthetic—the "real" Ahab does not connect flesh to flesh.

By reading scenes in *Moby-Dick* through some language theorists, particularly Austin and Butler for their theories of the force of language, this chapter demonstrates how Melville brings into focus the distinction between words and action so that speech stands as an active agent and, in fact, can act to resist the wounding that results from injurious language itself. Language theorists have claimed that persecutory language must be cited against itself, without reenacting injury. For example, to counter the injurious label of *queer,* the gay community has reclaimed and reappropriated that term, thereby reassigning it a positive value. *Queer* repeats a historically damaging slur without reenacting the damage. However, in *Moby-Dick,* Stubb devises a completely different strategy for countering the effects of Ahab's insult. Stubb does not reappropriate the damaging word *dog* nor rehabilitate the insults *donkey* and *ass.* He does not cite harmful language against itself. I expand upon Melville scholarship by demonstrating how *Moby-Dick* enacts a different strategy of resistance in order to disarm persecutory language. This linguistic strategy of action suggests that Melville meditates on language itself as prosthesis and understands that the status of language is tentative and that words and actions can become confused.

The conclusion addresses some current political situations in which the performativity of words determines citizenship and national leadership. I share a personal experience of a performative utterance that granted me citizenship and some questions that arise therefrom.

Performatively Speaking opens up the current critical conversation about antebellum American literature by asking readers to rethink the way that language and action intersect. While the first two chapters address the binding nature of performative language, the last three explore the way injurious language can be co-opted in order to performatively speak back and thus redress injury. By melding together literary theory, literary history, and close textual analysis, *Performatively Speaking* investigates moments where language, speech, or writing in fact function as action and demonstrate authors' awareness that words do not merely serve as description, sentimental suasion, or moral imperative, but rather have the volatility and power to injure, restrain, bind, or inaugurate a new identity. Over a hundred years before theorists codified performatives as such, the authors in my study seem to ask the question posed by Richard van Oort at the end of the twentieth century: "Are we representing a reality external to our utterance, or are we creating by the *very act of the utterance* the reality which we seek to define?" (n.p.). The writers discussed in this book agree that since the performative constitutes a discursive action, an utterance in fiction produces the very condition it names at the moment it is uttered, with compelling results.

1

Slave Promises and the Temperance Pledge

Written contracts arose amidst the decreasing faith placed in the oral promise. Before the rise of the legal system, a handshake sealed an agreement. In an increasingly litigious society, and with the expansion of commerce and more complicated trade arrangements, written agreements and contracts became more common in order to hold people to their word.

Yet interpersonal promises can bind as surely, and perhaps even more strongly, than standard legal contracts. Promises can be viewed as social rituals that bind or connect, but emotionally and psychically they constitute so much more. A broken contract can incur financial penalties, but a broken personal promise can damage even more extensively. For example, a lover's breach of faith might gouge at someone's heart more fiercely than a legal breach gouges at a wallet.

To some theorists, a promise points towards the future: according to Elizabeth Duquette, "Rather than questions of accuracy of verisimilitude, oaths or promises give voice to concerns about the importance of the future to the past, diminishing distinctions between history and fantasy while establishing obligations between people across time and space" (9). Likewise, Brook Thomas asserts the future orientation of the act of promising: "One enters into a promise because its terms cannot be immediately fulfilled. A promise's delivery is, in other words, by nature deferred. Indeed, once the promise has been delivered, the parties involved are no longer in the act of promising. As an interpersonal exchange, a promise is not simply made and then delivered or not delivered. Instead, contracting parties remain bound together, suspended in the act of promising, until the promise is delivered" (288). It may be true that there is a time lapse between making a promise and fulfilling it. However, the *act* of promising is instantaneous.

A promise is performative: when an individual utters "I promise to" or "I promise that," he or she engages in the act of promising. Saying something is not always simply stating a fact or describing an object; as Austin formulates his foundational theory, in performative speech "to *say* something is to *do* something" (12). Austin argues that promises constitute "explicit performatives," as opposed to "implicit performatives." He argues that explicit performatives "begin with or include some highly significant and unambiguous expression such as 'I bet,' 'I promise,' 'I bequeath'—an expression very commonly also used in naming the act which, in making such an utterance, I am performing—for example, betting, promising, bequeathing" (32). Thus, "I promise" is not a constative statement that notes the existence of a promise; rather, the phrase instantiates and enacts a condition of obligation. No time lapse exists between stating "I promise" and doing the act of promising; they are one and the same.

This chapter will explore selected moments of promising to investigate the way some mid-nineteenth-century American writers theorized the force of the act of voluntary verbal self-binding. Promises abound in literature, and therefore any literary investigation will necessarily be selective. For example, in Stowe's *Uncle Tom's Cabin,* Augustine St. Clare promises to free Tom, and George Shelby promises to buy Tom out of slavery and pledges his silver dollar as a sign of his promise and its partial fulfillment on Legree's plantation. In Melville's *Moby-Dick,* Queequeg makes a serious pledge of friendship by pressing his forehead to Ishmael's. Ahab swears an oath in "The Quarter Deck," and his proclamation that "the deed is done" implies an irrevocable action. In Harriet Jacobs's *Incidents in the Life of a Slave Girl,* Linda Brent tells readers that her grandmother's mistress promised to free her grandmother but died without ever doing so. Further, the mistress "borrowed" $300 from Linda's grandmother with a promise to pay it back but defaulted on that promise as well. Jacobs writes, "The reader probably knows that no promise or writing given to a slave is legally binding; for according to Southern laws, a slave, being property, can hold no property. When my grandmother lent her hard earnings to her mistress, she trusted solely to her honor. The honor of a slaveholder to a slave!" (6).

Sometimes people make promises *not* to engage in a certain action. For example, in Hannah Crafts's *The Bondswoman's Narrative,* Mr. Trappe tries to extort a promise from Mrs. Vincent, who refuses, saying "I will not bind myself" (41). Likewise, Mrs. Henry cannot solve Hannah's problems by buying her in order to then emancipate her because Mrs. Henry had long ago promised never to traffic in humans (127).

Although marriage vows are performative, I deliberately do not address them because such vows are litigable—their purview encompasses the force of the law. By uttering "I do" in a wedding ceremony, an individual engages in the act of consenting and agreeing to a legal contract. When the cleric or officiant states something along the lines of "I hereby pronounce you husband and wife" or "By the powers invested in me I hereby pronounce you married," the officiant does not comment on the fact that the couple seem to be married; he or she ushers the condition of wedlock into being by stating the right words in a proper context.

We understand that when we see a wedding ceremony on TV, in a movie, or on stage, the couple is not really getting married night after night. As Austin argues, for a performative to be successful, "There must exist an accepted conventional procedure having a certain conventional effect, the procedure to include the uttering of certain word by certain persons in certain circumstances" (26). Austin's conditions of felicity fail without a seriousness of intent if actors do not purposefully make a promise to each other. Austin terms such untruthful promises "misfires" or "misapplications." Thus, actors simulating a marriage are not truthfully engaging in a vow or promise and thus do not feel the bonds of interpersonal obligation. In a real wedding ceremony, after the vows have been made and the officiant has performatively enacted the condition of marriage, the newlyweds are bound by law as well as by a personal pledge. To undo the marriage requires many legal documents and much money. For these reasons, this chapter will focus on extrajudicial vows or promises, ones that bind personally or morally, not juridically.[1]

Slave Promises

I would like to focus on a particular subcategory of the promise that we find in antebellum American literature, one that reinforces human bondage and yet simultaneously offers opportunities for resistance: the slave's voluntary promise to his or her master. Slaves of course were not permitted to enter into legal contracts and thus could not sign agreements or even marry (although some masters permitted their slaves to hold wedding ceremonies, such marriages were not recognized by the state). If a slave uttered a vow to his or her master with sincerity of intention, such a promise cannot be considered a misfire or misapplication. Even though they might not be citizens legally recognized in the social contract, slaves often felt bound by their word even when it was given to an enslaving white master.

The act of promising sets up a curious condition for one legally held in bondage. The U.S. judicial system upheld slavery by the force of signatures on legal documents, but the slaves themselves could only be objects of exchange within contracts, never the signing subject. Slaves could be sold from one master to another by the promise of a sale or barter, but could not promise themselves in marriage or in their own private commercial enterprise. For example, Harriet Beecher Stowe's character George Harris in *Uncle Tom's Cabin* invents a machine for cleaning hemp, which his former master, Mr. Wilson, describes as "a really valuable affair; it's gone into use in several factories" (96). However, Mr. Wilson acknowledges that George Harris does not financially benefit from his own invention: according to Mr. Wilson, George's master holds the patent of it. Because he cannot enter his own labor into a contract, George can only be part of the machine he invents that enriches the man who owns both George and the rights to the hemp-cleaning machine.[2]

In *The Social Contract* (1762), Jean-Jacques Rousseau describes promises as equitable agreements between people, or between a person and the state: "The act of association consists of a reciprocal commitment between society and the individual, so that each person, in making a contract, as it were, with himself, finds himself doubly committed, first as a member of the sovereign body in relation to individuals, and secondly as a member of the state in relation to the sovereign" (quoted in Bannett 332). Nina Bannett rightly points out that Rousseau's formulation omits women since they did not retain independent legal status at the time; in fact, women's "first and last binding contract" was the marriage contract. Once women entered into marriage, they surrendered much of their legal existence and their independence to their husbands (Bannett 333). The next chapter discusses Fanny Fern's heroine Ruth Hall in relation to publishing contracts and how Ruth retains control over her legal representation since she does not have a husband to whom she must defer. Similar to white women, slaves found themselves outside the social contract since they could not willingly enter into a legally binding agreement as subjects; the bounds of white society defined by a social contract did not apply to them.

Despite lack of legal standing, women developed what Cindy Weinstein terms a "paradigm of contract," by which she means that "individual family members have rights that must be guaranteed and protected and that these rights increasingly come to be understood in affective terms" (9). I am particularly interested in expanding this paradigm of contract to include a family's slaves because it allows us to see how promises function between owner and owned, between those recognized and enfranchised by the law and those who are not.

If the idea of forging a promise is performative in that it creates and substantiates a binding situation, then the one who promises feels bound by his or her word to adhere to the terms of the vow. The promissory utterance transforms the speaking subject into the object of the oath such that she is beholden to her own very words. Examining a mid-nineteenth-century essay written for an abolitionist publication can illuminate the binding performativity of the promise.

Samuel J. May's "The Heroic Slave-Woman"

Samuel May, one of the nineteenth century's leading Unitarian ministers and an untiring social and educational reformer, wrote an essay called "The Heroic Slave-Woman" that appeared immediately preceding Frederick Douglass's *The Heroic Slave* in the 1853 abolitionist gift book *Autographs for Freedom*. May's essay favorably gives voice to a woman and her trustworthiness, which is especially welcome in light of Douglass's short novel that occludes women's agency (indeed, Susan, the wife of the novel's hero Madison Washington, remains mute throughout the story). But May's essay really concerns the determination of a white lawyer to understand the motivation of a black woman who remains unnamed. His essay dwells on the slave woman's undeviating promise to a white woman as well as on the white attorney Edward Abdy's inability to convince the slave woman to run to freedom while she has the chance. I would like to examine May's essay to explore the ways the slave woman's promise fastens and binds her to the very mistress from whom she wants liberation.

"The Heroic Slave-Woman" opens with the first-person voice of Reverend May describing his acquaintanceship with the English lawyer Edward S. Abdy, who received a commission from the British government to study the prison system in the United States. According to May, Abdy was more fascinated by the U.S. slavocracy system. In "The Heroic Slave-Woman," May writes that Abdy "travelled extensively in our Southern States, and contemplated with his own eyes the manifold abominations of our American despotism. He was too much exasperated by our tyranny to be enamoured of our democratic institutions" (161).

While May and Abdy sit at May's study window at his home in Connecticut, they see a carriage pull up to the hotel across the road carrying a white Mississippian couple with two children and a slave woman. May and Abdy dash over to speak with the slave owner, who defends the peculiar institution but offers the two gentlemen the opportunity to persuade his slave to claim her liberty while in the North. Eagerly May and Abdy try to convince the woman she is free; they cite cases and quote authorities as proof. However, the slave responds that she would not claim her freedom because, she says, "I *promised* mistress that I would go back with her and children" (163). May writes that Abdy argues with the woman and tells her "that such a promise was not binding" (163). In an ironic turn of phrase about captivity that refers to his companion being seized or held by an idea, May writes that Abdy is "possessed" by the spirit of William Paley's moral philosophy and thus cannot abide the woman not understanding that freedom is her due.

May writes that the slave woman "had bound herself by a promise to her mistress, that she would not leave her; and that promise had fastened upon her conscience and obligation, from which she could not be persuaded, that even her natural right to liberty could exonerate her" (163). Finally, Abdy becomes so infuriated with the woman's obstinate rejection of opportunity that he asks her if it might be the case that she did not want her freedom. The woman replies, "Was there ever a slave that did not wish to be free? I long for liberty. I will get out of slavery, if I can, the day after I have returned, but go back I must, because I *promised* that I would" (163). The next morning Abdy again tries to convince the woman to claim her freedom. Instead, the woman gestures towards her mistress's trunk and to a gold watch and chain that the mistress had entrusted to her and "insisted that fidelity to a trust was of more consequence to her soul even than the attainment of liberty" (164). In a final desperate offer to pry the woman loose from the bonds of her promise, Abdy offers to deliver the trunk to the master in the South personally so that the slave can remain in the free states. Again, the woman replies that she had promised she would return herself to her mistress and as "much as she longed for liberty, she longed for a clear conscience more" (164).

I am very interested in the conflation of two types of bondage here: one is government-sanctioned and carries the force of law while the other is interpersonal and spiritual. The slave woman in May's essay could easily break the legal bonds of slavery, but the personal bonds of her promise fasten her irrevocably tighter to her owner.

Because the slave woman's promise to her mistress occurs before the scene described in May's essay, we as readers do not witness the moment when she utters the words that compel her to return from Connecticut to Mississippi. However, we can assume that the mistress directly asked her servant to promise to return to the South from the North and that the slave uttered some phrase that included the performative "I promise." According to Austin, "The outward utterance is a description, *true or false,* of the occurrence of the inward performance. . . . Thus 'I promise to' obliges me—puts on record my spiritual assumption of a spiritual shackle" (9–10). Thus, although the slave woman may in her heart of hearts truly want her freedom, she outwardly uttered a promise that obviates her claiming her freedom without fulfilling her word.

Although the slave may have had to tamp down anger at her mistress and a deep desire to escape, her utterance exemplifies J. Hillis Miller's claim that "whatever we were thinking when we said it, what we say binds us" (32). Despite whatever ruminations the slave had about desiring freedom when she uttered her promise, she evidently did mean to stick to her word. Austin casts such an idea in terms of intention of performativity: "In the particular case of promising, as with many other performatives, it is appropriate that the person uttering the promise should have a certain intention, viz. here to keep his word" (11). That is, the slave indubitably thought one thing while performatively intending another. She craved release from bondage but bound herself anew. Ironically, deciding to keep her promise is one way the slave could achieve self-determination under slavery. In other words, although the slave woman felt bound by her promise, she exerted her own agency to adhere to her self-empowered word.

Judith Butler theorizes, however, that a promise is still performed even if the speaker had false pretenses: "Although a good intention may well make a promise felicitous, an intention not to perform the act does not deprive the speech act of its status as a promise; the promise is still performed. The force of the speech act is separable from its meaning and illocutionary force is secured through convention" (24). Following Butler's logic, even if the slave woman made a false promise of loyalty to her mistress, the performativity of the promise still inheres; the intention behind it does not deprive the utterance of a felicitous application. No matter what contradictory background thoughts the slave woman had, her promise still executed correctly.

All of this theorizing about the validity or felicitous execution of a promise raises the question of whether a slave woman can even make a contractual oath. As discussed above, a slave did not have the legal standing to enter into a contractual relation with another. Contractual principles presuppose a possessive individualism inaccessible to slaves. The so-called "peculiar institution" of slavery, while denying slaves the right to claim their own humanity, nonetheless held them accountable to their word.

Perhaps something else that vexed Abdy about a slave woman making a promise to her mistress is the assumed reciprocity of subjective equality inherent in the promise. In other words, in order for the slave woman to promise to return to the South with her mistress's trunks and jewels, some sort of intersubjective connection must take place between the free and the chained. According to Thomas, "The subjective theory of contract assumes that a promise is made the moment there is a meeting of the minds of two already-formed individuals" (287). This theory of contract would then require that the Mississippian slave could be viewed as an "already-formed individual" who had a mind that could meet that of her mistress. Thomas also remarks that the very structure of promising requires some "fusion of subjectivities" between the promissory parties (288). Further, according to Thomas, "Once a promise is made it creates a future obligation. Promising so conceived becomes a moral act itself rather than one simply recording an obligation created by the mysterious merger of two autonomous wills" (287). The performative act of promising verges into the realm of morality since it entwines the expectations of two people.

Abdy undoubtedly found himself vexed and delighted that the slave woman he observed had such a fine-tuned sense of morality, which therefore indicated her sense of individuality and her autonomous will. The slave woman seems to have found that making a promise serves as a measure of liberation: committing herself to such an action is predicated on her first claiming agency. By engaging in a promise, the slave woman resists the prevailing legal and moral ideology that denies her the standing to engage in any form of contract. Therefore, although her promise to return south might seem antithetical to achieving freedom, the very act of making and adhering to the promise self-authorizes agency and subjectivity and thereby grants the woman a measure of liberty to determine her future.

Yet here we see a slave inaugurating the very condition that binds her to another. Miller discusses how performative speech acts, when first articulated as such by Austin, were understood to exclude nonfelicitous utterances such as jokes, satirical comments, or theatrical situations on the stage (79). To subordinate the nonserious to the serious, Austin likely imagined the speaking *I* who would inaugurate a promise to be an "ego, or subject, a person, ideally male, in full possession of his senses, speaking in the present with deliberate intention, and uttering 'I promise so and so.' Then come all the impure promises as deviations from that, for example promises imitated in a novel, or acted on the staged, or said with intent not to keep them, or under coercion, or by someone who is insane or drugged, or someone from a culture that does not share our assumptions about promises" (80). Although Austin does not mention the male speaker's race or class, the heroine of May's "The Heroic Slave-Woman" likely contradicts all of Austin's assumptions about who utters promises, and embodies "secondary, impure, etiolated, fictive deformations of real promises" (Miller 80). Since her slave status (not to mention her being female and black) renders her identity to be secondary or subordinate, the slave woman's promissory utterance is somehow nonserious and "impure." Any slave promise certainly would not hold up in a white court of law, but, as we have seen, the slave woman of May's account believes in the legitimate, contractual value of her pledge.

Jacques Derrida, however, inverts the pure/impure hierarchy so that a promise is not derived from a "pure" state to begin with; he argues that vows originate from an impure state because, in Miller's paraphrase, "what exists 'originally' are speech acts marked, from the beginning or even before the beginning, by iterability, that is, by impurity. The impure is the original. The pure, normal, standard speech act, if there were such a thing, would be derived from that" (80). In other words, in order to be understandable and thus felicitous, all words in a promise must have been used before; they repeat the convention of stating "I promise" using preexisting, pre-packaged words. The words *I promise* must be iterable, must repeat a pre-established pattern of verbal exchange in order to conform to a binding script. The very nature of their iterability testifies to their unoriginality. Thus, following Derrida, the slave woman of May's essay no more utters an impure promise than any upper-class white man such as May or Abdy. Her words should be just as binding as theirs. Abdy and May's fascination with her pledge reveals their moral blindness—they fail to see the white privilege that claims pure intention of language.

Given that the Mississippian slave woman's promise exists, why can't she break it? What prevents her from prioritizing her own freedom over another woman's luggage and jewels? Why does the slave woman feel so beholden to her mistress if, according to the slave's later revelation to Abdy, she desperately desires emancipation and likely had contradictory thoughts when uttering her binding words? If the slave woman enacted her own bondage through her performative utterance, why can't she verbally unbind herself as well? Why are a slave woman's words more inescapable than a government decree? These constitute the very questions that most puzzle Abdy. At the end of "The Heroic Slave-Woman," May writes that, "We could not but feel a profound respect for that moral sensibility which would not allow her to embrace even her freedom, at the expense of violating a promise" (163). For the slave woman, the moral and spiritual self-binding hold faster than the bonds of slavery, which could easily be severed by simply remaining in Connecticut. To her, a clear connection exists between her word and her moral obligation.

Abdy is so "astonished, delighted at this instance of heroic virtue in a poor, ignorant slave" that he packs his own bag, says goodbye to Reverend May, and sits with the bondswoman on the outside of the coach headed to Mississippi in order to "study for a few hours more the morality of that strong-hearted woman, who could not be bribed to violate her promise, even by the gift of her liberty" (164). May's contribution to *Autographs for Freedom* concludes with his musing, "It was the last time I saw Mr. Abdy,—and it was a sight to be remembered,—he an accomplished English gentleman, a Fellow of Oxford or Cambridge University, riding on the driver's box of a stage-coach, side by side with an American slave-woman, that he might learn more of her history and character" (164).

The slave who embodies a "heroic virtue" that inspires Abdy to ride a wagon south and that inspires May to turn the incident into an essay for an abolitionist publication also exemplifies a "moral sensibility" beyond the reach of the educated white elite. May and Abdy's delight and perplexity seem to derive from the yawning gulf between "heroic virtue"/"moral sensibility" and "poor ignorant slave." The implication is that only someone ignorant could willingly surrender freedom; thus, some special spiritual force or insight must be at work. Is this what made "The Heroic Slave-Woman" an appealing choice as an antislavery activist piece for inclusion in *Autographs for Freedom*?

British abolitionist Julia Griffiths traveled from England to Rochester, New York, in 1849 to live with Frederick Douglass, whom she had met during his tour of the British Isles from 1845-47, in order to help fundraise for, manage, and edit his newspapers. She served as secretary of the Rochester Ladies' Anti-Slavery Society and edited the gift book *Autographs for Freedom* to raise money for the society. As with other gift books that published annually, Griffiths intended to issue a volume of *Autographs* every year, but only the 1853 and 1854 editions were published, both in time for the holiday seasons. But Griffiths returned to England in 1855 after William Lloyd Garrison accused her and Douglass of having an extra-marital affair, although she continued her abolitionist and fundraising activities from abroad.

Autographs for Freedom stands among several abolitionist literary annuals. For example, Maria Weston Chapman edited the *Liberty Bell* for almost two decades, and various editors annually produced the *Oasis*. As women more and more served as gift book editors, they could recast "women's agency within the gift books' characteristically asymmetrical systems of exchange" (McGill 198). Such gift books of the 1830s and 1840s "paved the way for women's domination of the market for sentimental fiction in the 1850s" (ibid.).

"The Heroic Slave-Woman" seems an appropriate choice for the genre of the gift book in general. While some have considered antebellum annuals to be "ornamental, light, frivolous, and escapist" (Lehuu 77), more recent critics have recognized the complex and significant role that gift books played in antebellum print culture.[3] According to Isabel Lehuu, a gift book was "in fact far more than a book. It was primarily a gift and a sign of taste and social status" (ibid.). As luxury goods, literary annuals featured fine binding, gilt lettering, and enlightened content. Giving or receiving one highlighted refined bourgeois taste and suggested emotional intimacy between the giver and the receiver. Rather than being hidden among many tomes on a shelf, gift books were publicly displayed on a table in a middle-class parlor. According to Karen Halttunen, the parlor was a mediating space between the "urban street and the more private rooms of the house. The parlor represented a woman's 'cultural podium' where she would exert her influence. . . . Giftbooks too were consumer goods that helped define the middle-class households and demonstrate good taste—that is, moral standing" (quoted in Lehuu 84).

Why would Reverend May's essay about the double binding of a slave's promise, and a white Englishman's fascination with it, find a place in Griffiths's and Douglass's abolitionist anthology? We might never know the actual reasons about specific editorial decisions, but we can make educated guesses based on the genre of the gift book.

Although Abdy does not write about this Philadelphia incident with Samuel May and the Mississippian bondwoman in the book he subsequently published about his travels in the United States, he discusses an analogous incident of a slave who travels to Philadelphia with his owner. The slave owner returns south in advance of his slave, from whom he has exacted a promise to return in due time. The slave tells his sister that he intends to break the vow to return south and instead remain in the free North. Upset by this violation of his word, the slave's sister reportedly says, "If he does so . . . he shall never enter my house again. Whatever may be his wrongs, his honor ought not to be forfeited." Based on this and other incidents, Abdy comments that slave loyalty "is so general, and so well understood, that masters often allow their slaves to go into other States, upon their promising not to abscond" (3:352). Abdy further evidences his interest in the idea of promising when in his journal he addresses the faithfulness of the Tuscarora Indians: "So great is the confidence reposed in their honesty, that their word is sufficient security for the payment of a debt or the performance of a promise; no written agreement being even required of them" (1:316).

Besides being paired with Douglass's *The Heroic Slave*, "The Heroic Slave-Woman" stands out in *Autographs for Freedom* for another reason: the volume contains a frontispiece engraving and only two additional pictorial engravings, one of which illustrates a scene from "The Heroic Slave-Woman."[4] Of all the contributions in the volume, "The Heroic Slave-Woman" is one of only two pieces that are accompanied by a picture.[5]

The illustration shows two white gentlemen in formal attire and top hats speaking to a black woman dressed in humble clothes and a head wrap. One of the gentlemen is gesturing towards the woman as he speaks, and the woman is pointing to a large trunk on the ground next to her. The background is sparse, but with a bench and posters on the wall saying "Stage," the scene likely takes place in an outdoors waiting area for a stagecoach. After reading the accompanying story, it seems evident that the man gesturing towards the woman is Abdy and that the engraving illustrates the moment when he tries to convince her to remain in the North. By gesturing towards the trunk, the woman indicates her obligation to stay and see the trunk safely back to Mississippi. The other gentleman in the picture therefore must be the author, Samuel May.

While a pictorial grouping of the three personalities in the story may seem unexceptional, the representation of the female slave plays a different role in the history of gift book illustration. According to Lehuu, early literary annuals predominantly featured engravings of the sea, of historical events, of landscapes, and of genre painting. As gift books became more important to women readers, female portraiture appeared more often. Since, according to Lehuu, "men far outnumbered women in portrait collections of the nineteenth century," thus "the importance of female portraiture in gift books is particularly striking" (93–94). If the presence of illustrations of women was intended to communicate familiarity and consonance with female readers, then black portraiture suggests a certain sisterhood among white readers and black women featured in the engraving. Young women were often featured in annuals' illustrations because they were the main consumers of the genre. As Lehuu points out, "Because of their exclusion from economic competition, women were thought to be the moral guardians of American society and the angel in the house, albeit a consuming angel" (100). In addition, engravings incurred significant costs for gift books; some publishers often paid more for one engraving than the combined cost of all the literary content (Patterson 138).

A final point to mention pertaining to the significance of the illustration accompanying "The Heroic Slave-Woman" is that clusters of three women often appeared in gift books to signify the conjoining of the sister arts of painting, poetry, and music, as well as the three graces connected with gift books—giving, receiving, and returning. Thus, the engraving featuring the trio of Abdy, May, and the Mississippian slave woman presents a comfortable trinity that would resonate with middle-class women readers and yet would challenge received genteel notions that excluded black portraiture or the presence of black women in literary annuals. The engraving accompanying "The Heroic Slave-Woman," then, both draws attention to the essay and announces intersubjective identification between white and black women.

Since *Autographs for Freedom* specifically aimed to raise money for the abolitionist cause, all of the contributors donated their pieces without receiving payment. The last page of each contribution contains an engraving of the writer's autograph as a stand-in for his or her presence. Reverend Samuel J. May's signature at the end of "The Heroic Slave-Woman" attests to truths or beliefs about the incident conveyed in his account. The story seems appropriate for an abolitionist gift book because the Mississippian slave woman, a curiosity to Edward Abdy, demonstrates that keeping a promise can be heroic and that it indicates the ability to claim self-agency and self-governance. The slave woman becomes a model for young women readers as she demonstrates her self-authorized capacity for constancy and faithfulness. Just as Abdy and May admire the slave woman for her loyalty, so, too, does she prove all slaves' potential for loyalty and honorable action, which would argue in favor of emancipation. Although the Mississippian slave woman is legally bound to her mistress, "The Heroic Slave-Woman" shifts the idea of power as the owner becomes beholden to the owned to keep her oath to return south. The performativity of the slave's promise demonstrates intersubjective bonds beyond the reach of the juridical system and thus substantiates beliefs that bondsmen and bondswomen deserved their freedom.

The Performativity of the Temperance Vow

Because of unsanitary water conditions, and because of accepted social norms, Americans in the eighteenth and nineteenth centuries drank large quantities of alcohol daily. Workers often drank beer or wine while on the job; for example, Benjamin Franklin writes in his *Autobiography* (1771) that his coworkers would pay an alehouse boy to bring them fresh beer several times a day in the belief that strong beer built strong bodies. According to scholarly estimates, the average U.S. citizen in 1830 drank an astounding seven gallons of pure alcohol per year. However, a century and a half later in 1985, American drinking consumption had declined to only 2.6 gallons per person annually (Lender and Martin 95).

What accounts for such a dramatic reduction in the consumption of alcohol? Improvements in water purification certainly made water a safer option as the nineteenth century progressed, but this technological innovation alone cannot account for Americans switching their allegiance from the keg tap to the kitchen tap. In fact, the moral suasion techniques and increased legal action of the temperance movement played an enormous role in convincing people to put down the bottle.

The temperance crusade expanded in the early nineteenth century and swept through the country as a result of the nation's long history of alcoholic overindulgence. The temperance movement, contemporaneous with abolition, women's suffrage, and with the development of the railroad and the telegraph, was possibly the largest social movement in the nineteenth century. While antislavery reform first began in Britain and spread across the ocean to the United States, the anti-alcohol movement actually began in the U.S. and then took hold in Britain. The anti-liquor effort culminated with Prohibition, made law by the Eighteenth Amendment to the U.S. Constitution in 1919, which made self-control and public virtue into issues of national interest. Supporters thus believed that morality could and should be legislated.

Those involved in the national movement to stop Americans from drinking had many concerns. They asserted that alcohol enslaved the drinker's body and will, just as African Americans who were legally enslaved did not hold control of their body or will. In his *Narrative of the Life of Frederick Douglass,* Douglass describes the way slaveholders robbed their slaves of dignity and independence by forcing them to drink themselves into a stupor during holidays; Douglass concludes that he and fellow slaves "had almost as well be slaves to man as to rum" (91). In his speech "Intemperance and Slavery: An Address Delivered in Cork, Ireland, on October 20, 1845," Douglass twinned the enslaving aspects of bondage and inebriation by arguing that "if we could but make the world sober, we would have no slavery."

Temperance advocates further argued that heavy drinking caused men to lose their jobs and thereby impoverish their families, that inebriation directly led to poor health, and that, furthermore, drunkenness indicated a sinful life.

The Washingtonian temperance group, founded in Baltimore in 1840, held support meetings at which drinkers shared aloud stories of their experiences and formed encouraging and salvific bonds as they recognized familiar patterns of behavior in fellow members, not unlike what occurred at evangelical revivals.[6] Thomas Augst argues that such public stories "turned the domestic lives of ordinary men into a new kind of public spectacle purveyed by temperance societies, fiction, drama, and the lecture hall" (298). Often, drinkers' testaments became ever more dramatic. Full of graphic descriptions of drunken nightmarish adventures and domestic violence, their titillating confessions drew ever more people to the movement. Washingtonian discourse was often violent and lurid in its renderings of alcohol's ravages, and people were eager to read and hear about the degeneracy and wickedness they supposedly protested. The Washingtonian phase, which extended in various forms until the early 1850s, had particular relevance to the development of American literature.[7]

The temperance movement enjoyed great success, even though its crowning achievement of Prohibition lasted only thirteen years before its repeal in 1933 with the Twenty-First Amendment. Even at the close of the nineteenth century, reformers looked back to the heyday of the Washingtonian movement as inspiration, as in an 1893 editorial from the *Chautauquan* magazine: "Men and women must take up the old-fashioned arguments in favor of total abstinence and prohibition and go before the public with the same arguments that our fathers used in the days of the Washingtonian movement. They must not despise the temperance pledge; they must ask men and women to pledge themselves to a life of temperance" ("Editor's Outlook" 355). The American Temperance Union, an organization devoted to the dry cause, recognized the capability of temperance fiction to disseminate anti-alcohol propaganda to large numbers of readers. In 1836 members voted to endorse the use of such literature, especially didactic tracts, to spread its message. The National Temperance Society became a publisher of temperance fiction, which assured it a public voice in the fight against intoxication.

The nineteenth-century temperance tale enjoyed success by generally sticking to a formula: a young innocent boy, often from the country, moves to the city in search of work, has his first drink of alcohol, and rapidly degenerates into an unrepentant drunkard who impoverishes his family and dies inebriated. Elaine Parsons identifies six key features of drunk narratives: 1) the young male protagonist is particularly promising; 2) he falls due to external influences; 3) he is weak-willed and too eager to please his new friends; 4) his desire for drink overwhelms all else; 5) he loses control of his family, money, and body; and 6) if he is redeemed, it is through powerful external influence (11).[8] Of course, not all temperance tales follow this formula; some, in fact, feature drunk women, and many feature the influential strength of supportive women.

Although we now have a medical model of alcoholism as a disease, the nineteenth century believed inebriation was a sign of moral weakness and the drinker to be a morally defective sinner. Anti-drink stories aimed to reveal to drunkards their unacceptable ways and show them how to lead a sober life blessed with economic security and familial love. In this chapter I want to explore what happens when the drunkard does not find redemption through what Parsons calls a "powerful external influence," but through the powerful self-binding internal force of the performative temperance pledge.

Just as Austin argues that for a performative to be felicitous there must be "the uttering of certain words by certain persons in certain circumstances" (14), temperance advocates hoped that the right words, told in the right way, could change the way society talked about itself and its values, how people saw themselves in relationship to alcohol, and what kind of citizens they hoped to be. In many temperance stories, the moment of the drunkard's redemption hinges on him signing or stating the temperance pledge.

Because alcohol enslaved the drunkard while the pledge emancipated him from drunkenness, temperance rhetoric often overlapped with abolitionist rhetoric. The temperance pledge can be seen as at once binding and liberating: it simultaneously shackles the drinker's actions and yet releases him from inebriation. Many abolitionists and women's suffrage advocates started as temperance workers; the conservative anti-alcohol movement did not seem antithetical to the progressive abolitionist and suffrage agitation because all three reform movements advocated for expanded liberties. Samuel May's "The Heroic Slave-Woman" reflects the dual nature of the pledge or promise as both fettering and liberating: the eponymous heroine's promise irrevocably ties her to her mistress, yet honoring a promise offers the slave woman a unique opportunity to resist slavery's dehumanization and to claim self-agency.

This remainder of this chapter will explore the paradoxical liberation that can come from the act of voluntary self-binding that results from the performative act of signing or stating the temperance pledge. To do that, I will examine the performativity of the utterances that bring sobriety to long-time drunkards. Much nineteenth-century temperance fiction features drunken men, particularly fathers, signing an oath of total temperance or abstinence as the moral climax of the story. This moment of conversion when the drunkard pledges to be sober brings readers and characters together in a shared moment of relief and deliverance. Such scenes rely on the efficacy of sentimental suasion; the American Temperance Union lauded and encouraged emotional, purple scenes that drew in readers.

The culminating statement of sobriety or signature on the temperance pledge is performative. That is, the utterance "I promise" or "I pledge" constitutes an action: when an individual utters "I promise to" or "I promise that," he or she engages in the very act of promising. Both phrases instantiate and enact a condition of obligation. The promissory utterance transforms the speaking subject into the very object of his or her words. In May's "The Heroic Slave-Woman," the Mississippian bondswoman understands the binding effect of a promise or pledge: she refuses the opportunity to seize freedom because she feels bound to honor her verbal commitment to her mistress.

The temperance vow, then, oscillates between sentimental feeling and performative action. Temperance stories attempt to manipulate the reader into feeling a certain way so that the performative moment of the pledge crowns a moral and sentimental achievement. The temperance pledge's embodiment of both affect and action raises many questions: how do the effects of performative speech differ from affective rhetoric? What does it mean for a speech act to be a speech feeling? Is the efficacy of sentiment indebted to the performativity? Or vice versa? Can the performativity of a temperance pledge redeem charges that its maudlin nature reeks of inauthenticity? Is it more powerful to appeal to performative force or to sentiment? When are they the same? What happens when theories about sentimentalism and speech act theory merge in the case of the temperance vow? Is one theory or genre indebted to another?

Various temperance pledges existed throughout the nineteenth century. Some short pledges foreswore only distilled liquor but permitted beer and wine. As beer and wine increased in popularity, many felt that total abstinence, or T-total refusal (which gave rise to the word *teetotaler*) alone could save drunkards. Long pledges refused medicinal alcohol (which often contained up to 40% alcohol) and communion wine. In the second part of the century the emphasis placed on pledges still stood, but reformers placed an even higher premium on trying to change laws that would regulate the sales of intoxicating beverages. Although most signers of the pledge committed to overhauling their drinking habits, some inscribed their names to confirm that they were already temperate and would only drink wine in moderation and abstain from liquor completely (Claybaugh 93).[9]

For example, in T. S. Arthur's "Flushed With Wine," the drunkard Harvey Lane, fearing he is about to die in a duel instigated when he insults his friend James Everett, reforms at the story's end and states, "From this hour, I solemnly declare, that I will never again touch, taste, or handle the accursed thing" (*Lights* 104). The story can resolve when Harvey realizes that his troubles stem from his unbounded drinking and declares his intent to abstain. The performative meets the sentimental in a highly charged climactic scene of personal and familial redemption.

In another of Arthur's stories, "The Failing Hope," James Martin makes an initial attempt at pledging sobriety. He tells his wife Emma, "I have resolved never again to touch the accursed cup that has so well-nigh destroyed our peace for ever" (ibid. 128). Martin goes to a dinner party "firm in his resolution not to touch a drop of ardent spirits" (130), but "the taste of wine . . . inflame[s] his appetite." He continues to drink "until he cease[s] to feel the power of his resolution, and again put[s] brandy to his lips" (ibid.). After years of degradation and the requisite formulaic tears and imploring of his wife and young daughter, Martin decides that only a vow of abstinence, not flexible temperance, will help him. For a second time Martin binds himself via the action of a pledge: "I have, therefore, most solemnly promised myself, that I will never again touch or taste any spirituous liquors, wine, malt, or cider. Nor will I again attend any convivial parties, where these things are used. Hereafter, I shall act upon the total-abstinence principle—for only in total-abstinence, is there safety for one like me" (138). With Martin performatively uttering the vow, the story can draw rapidly to a close: "Years have passed, since that total-abstinence resolution was taken, and not once during the time has Martin been tempted to violate it. Yet, is he vividly conscious, that only in *total-abstinence* from everything that can intoxicate is there safety for him" (139). In these instances, both Harvey Lane and James Martin utter promissory vows that enact new structures of self-shackling that lead to sobriety. The power of the utterance transforms them morally, socially, and behaviorally.

How does this occur? In the act of performatively uttering the temperance pledge not to drink, three things happen. First, the utterance "I promise" or "I pledge" constitutes an action that binds or restricts the speaker to his words. According to Austin, "'I promise to' obliges me—puts on record my spiritual assumption of a spiritual shackle" (10). Interestingly, the temperance pledge is a promise *not* to do something. It differs from a promise to pay a debt or to meet a deadline or to betroth oneself. Those are all promises to accomplish a deed, to do something. The temperance pledge, on the other hand, appears negative. It negates and refuses, binding the speaker to an oath *not* to engage in a future activity. However, at the level of speech act theory, the two types of promises are the same. The utterances "I promise/pledge to" and "I promise/pledge not to" constitute an action and instantiate and enact a condition of obligation, whether positive or negative.

Second, in the act of performatively uttering the temperance pledge not to drink, the alcohol becomes a forbidden object. The object of the vow becomes a prohibited substance. An ordinary object, such as a bottle of wine, transforms into taboo through the power of a performative utterance. Lydia Sigourney, in her 1834 volume *The Intemperate and the Reformed,* similarly casts the pledge in terms of totemic power: the "temperance pledge in the hour of temptation, is like the amulet worn of old to preserve its wearer from evils. The remembered pledge often exerts a saving power, when the waves of temptation beat violently against the trembling resolution of the reformed drunkard" (40–41).[10] In Walt Whitman's 1842 novel *Franklin Evans,* the title character initially signs a temperance pledge "which forb[ids] only the drinking of the most ardent kinds of liquors, and allow[s] people to get as much fuddled as they cho[o]se upon wine, and beer, and so on" (136). Thus, since the totemic power of the pledge makes only liquor taboo, Evans and his contemporaries are free to indulge in drinking nonprohibited beer and wine.

In another example of wine becoming a forbidden object from *The Intemperate and the Reformed,* Sigourney narrates the stories of thirty-eight village drunkards who become temperate. In one anecdote, she receives a visit from a drunk neighbor who wants to sign the temperance pledge. She writes it out for him to sign. "He took the pen, fell upon his knees, and signed it; and immediately after offered an audible prayer of ten minutes' length. Strange to say, he has never tasted spirituous liquor since" (36). In this case, signing the pledge assumes the power of an amulet, totem, or protective spell, and thus uttering the words or signing one's name to the words enacts the magical powers of prohibitionary action.

A danger of placing so much faith in the power of words to enact an embargo on behavior is that the power of one's words can be doubted. Many temperance writers portray failed attempts to keep the temperance pledge and the dangers that arise from moral laxity. For that reason, the temperance vow must be made in public; part of its power derives from having witnesses that make the promissory nature of the utterance even more binding. To nineteenth-century reformers, the temperance pledge is social and thus requires community.

Third, when reformers utter or sign the temperance pledge, they cite from a pre-existing script. Signers do not invent the pledge anew every time; rather they recite or repeat words that recall and repeat an established practice. Their utterance can felicitously work because the words in the pledge carry an embedded history of promising and sobriety. In Derridean terms, the temperance pledge exemplifies citation: it repeats words and drags along their original meaning (*Limited Inc* 12).[11] Were the drunkard to utter nonsense words or words that did not adhere to a recognized pattern of temperance pledges, the utterance would be considered, in Austinian terms, a misapplication, misinvocation, misexecution, or misfire (Austin 17).

According to Austin, a promise is predicated on an "outward and visible sign" of an "inward and spiritual act" (9). In other words, a serious promise must manifest truthful intention. Furthermore, a promise cannot be made secretly but must have an audience to solidify the link between utterance and authenticity. Miller expands on Austin: "The smooth working of society, of 'law and order,' depends, it can be argued, on ignoring whatever goes on secretly in people's hearts and holding them to the rule that says our word is our bond. . . . I must be in my right mind and not coerced. That, however, is not the same thing as saying my word is my bond" (31). For example, can one be held to a promise made ironically, that is, while saying one thing but meaning something else entirely (ibid. 42)? If you promise to pay your brand-loyal buddy a million dollars to try a new brand of beer, no one will really hold you to that deal. Irony undermines obligation; thus the temperance vow must be made with all seriousness of intention. For example, in Henrietta Rose's 1858 novel *Nora Wilmot*, Ernest makes lame attempts to stay sober: "Once he pledged himself again to drink no more; but this time his resolution was inadequate to the trial, and he again yielded, and turned, with a renewed energy, to the fatal cup" (31). Ernest's wife grieves her husband's lack of sincerity when vowing temperance and unsuccessfully tries "endeavoring by every means in her power to win him back, if possible, to the paths of rectitude and virtue" (317). Listeners, therefore, may doubt the ability of the swearer to follow through on the oath, although the pledge may have been uttered or signed felicitously.

For example, in a temperance address given in 1842 in Springfield, Illinois, Abraham Lincoln humorously poses the ironic question of die-hard drinkers: "What good can I do by signing the pledge? I never drink without signing." Lincoln projects the insincerity of those who outwardly declare themselves sober as a cover for their inward intention to drink heavily (not dissimilarly, Whitman evidently wrote his temperance novel *Franklin Evans* while drinking heartily[12]). In T. S. Arthur's story "The Temperance Pledge," Jane Jarvis similarly doubts the outward binding nature of her husband John Jarvis's word as she gives him another quarter for alcohol, weeping "you who pledged yourself" (*Lights* 56). This time, however, instead of drinking the money, John uses it to pay dues at the temperance society as his friend reads the constitution of the Washing-tonian temperance society in his town: "We, the undersigned, do pledge ourselves to each other, as gentlemen, that we will not, hereafter, drink any spirituous liquors, wine, malt, or cider, unless in sickness, and under the prescription of a physician" (58). John believes the performative act of pledging himself ensures sobriety. Potential employers, however, doubt his ability to stay straight. One refuses to offer him a job, saying, "I am afraid of you, John. You are such an old offender on the score of drunk-enness, that I have no confidence in your power to keep the pledge" (61). The employer identifies a schism between John's outward and visible act of pledging and his inward and private intention or potential.

In *The Intemperate and the Reformed*, Sigourney anticipates Austin's contention about the need for the pledge to be made outward and vis-ible, and she similarly emphasizes that the pledge needs to be made in public, as opposed to being sworn in private, in order to be effective: "Nothing, however, has been so useful, towards effecting, and especially towards rendering permanent, the reformation of drunkards here, as the public pledge, which the temperance society requires of its members" (40). Sigourney goes on to illuminate the effectiveness of the pledge's public nature:

> The pledge associates him with the respectable, who have subscribed it; and he feels himself honored by the association, and stimulated to well doing. This public promise constitutes, in his view, whatever it may be in fact, a far more solemn appeal to the living God than do his private and, generally, vague and hesitating resolutions of amendment; and he is also most profitably conscious, that this public promise fixes upon

him the eyes of hundreds of his fellow beings, who will stand ready to applaud him for his fidelity to it, or to despise and abhor its violation." (ibid.)

She anecdotally cites one drunkard who publically signed the pledge so that "now that he had taken upon himself the obligations of a pledge, an oath, in very truth, binding the nobler part of his manly nature, his friends had much to hope" (63–64). In Glenn Hendler's terms, temperance pledges are "attempts to shape what might later be seen as private experience into something social—or, to use a more historically and theoretically specific term, into something *public*" (128). Such public experience meetings, which featured oral narratives as preludes to the performativity of the pledge, all constitute the public sphere.

Henrietta Rose imagines the family in *Nora Wilmot* as comprising the public site that seals a promissory bond: "Charley made a full acknowledgment of his whole course of dissipation to his good wife, and, of course, she forgave it all; and then he drew up a pledge of entire abstinence, now, henceforth, and forever, signed it himself, together with his wife, and intends to have his children sign it, the first intelligible word they ever write" (283). Amanda Claybough argues that many temperance plots are plots of "double promising," where the marriage vow and temperance vow inextricably intertwine because the wife needs the temperance pledge to sustain her husband's marriage vows (96).[13] Arthur similarly depicts the efficacy of a public audience when signing the pledge in "The Drunkard's Wife." Dr. Harper is so moved upon hearing a temperance speaker that he "subscribed his name to the pledge" (*Temperance* 2:2). The story then flashes back to account for what brought him to the space of a public meeting. In Caroline Lee Hentz's "The Drunkard's Daughter," we do not see Mr. Franklin take the temperance pledge, but his public desire to "prove the sincerity of [his] reformation" (109) is enough to vindicate his name and thus free Katie, the drunkard's daughter of the story's title, to marry her suitor Harry Blake.

Hendler theorizes the public space of telling one's story and performatively uttering the pledge as a site of constructing both masculinity and whiteness. Through a shared nonhierarchical experience of confessing failure and violence as husbands or providers, men reinforce a communal identity markedly different from that experienced by women (125). Furthermore, Hendler argues that "Washingtonian whiteness and masculinity are constructed through a dialectic of identification and disavowal; the drunkard, and those who sympathize with him, become white men by dissolving their bodies in tears. The temperance story provides a narrative form for that process, restructuring the ambiguous affective responses embodied in the figure of the alcoholic and transforming them into a more legible sentimental experience" (142). The public space of the drunk narrative and the uttering of the pledge was further masculinized by the fact that women were not allowed to speak in experience meetings or tell their stories of abuse at the hands of drunk men (ibid. 137).

Experience meetings and temperance pledges also constructed whiteness in the way drunken men linked their inebriation to enslavement. By using their will and a publicly witnessed speech act to self-liberate from the shackles of alcohol, drunkards reinforced a definition of freedom informed by white privilege. For example, in Rose's novel *Nora Wilmot,* Nora believes that her father "took the same side of many well meaning men in those days, who were honestly mistaken in their views, that, in giving a signature to a pledge of abstinence, they would be bartering their liberties—yielding a portion of their precious boon of freedom" (60). Eventually, however, "with a manly independence . . . he at once shook off the manacles that bound him and stepped forth a free man, with his name enrolled as a member of one of the most strenuous associations for the suppression of intemperance" (63).[14]

In addition to having ramifications for masculine and white identity, the performativity of the public temperance pledge could also support class identity. Choice of drink has always been associated with various ethnic and class identities. For example, Nora's father in *Nora Wilmot* runs for political office as a "son of Erin" and during the campaign season "[makes] use of the social glass as a means of increasing his popularity with one class of voters. Dram drinking was not then so entirely unpopular with the better portions of society; ardent spirits were used to some extent in all classes" (59). By tapping into his Irish identity, Nora's father encodes a certain type of drinking pattern with middle-class aspiration and performs an upwardly mobile Irish identity in the public sphere in order to garner votes.

The original Washingtonians formed from the working class who wanted to achieve sobriety as part of an effort to secure middle-class respectability. The performative act of promising meant that such men could be held accountable to their word; they were not suspicious, unaccountable men unworthy of being trusted with employment and good judgment. Brook Thomas questions whether a promise can legitimate social and economic inequality by referring to Sir Henry Maine's idea, expressed in his 1861 treatise *Ancient Law,* that societies have progressed by moving "from Status to Contract." Thomas writes, "For Maine, traditional societies determined people's duties and obligations according to status. For instance, in medieval society both peasant and lord were assigned clear-cut, if different, duties and obligations according to the hierarchical social class into which each was born. In contrast, contractual societies undermine those hierarchies by determining duties and obligations through negotiations among contracting parties" (2). Thomas further cites William Graham Sumner as saying, "A society based on contract, therefore, gives the utmost room and chance for individual development, and for all the self-reliance and dignity of a free man. . . . That the only social improvements which are now conceivable lie in the direction of more complete realization of a society of free men united by contract, are points which cannot be controverted" (quoted in Thomas 3). A pledge of temperance, then, can undo the hierarchy of class by enacting a moral and social change in the former drunkard and raise his status level.

I asserted earlier that the temperance vow, while performative, also depended for its success on sentimental feeling. Experience meetings in which drunkards told tales of woe before signing the pledge mandated that the public audience sentimentally identify and emotionally bond with the drunkard in his moment of conversion. The temperance pledge thus embodies both affect and action, virtually doubling the speech act as a speech feeling. At the same time, critics of maudlin sentimentality contend that the purple, didactic, and formulaic nature of the pledge signifies inauthenticity as temperance stories draw upon a clichéd and prepackaged stage setting that predetermines readers' emotions.[15] However, the reader can only fully trust the weeping wife and child or the reforming drunkard if the sentimental moment of the vow of temperance is sincere or authentic. The performative nature of the temperance vow—the way that it enacts and inaugurates its own existence—perhaps increases the authenticity of the moment. In other words, the action-based condition of a performative promise means that not just sentiment is at work: the temperance pledge effects results because of its reliance on action, not just feeling. Theories about sentimentalism and speech act theory merge in the temperance vow as we see that the success of the sentimental moment may be indebted to the performativity of speech and that to be felicitous, the temperance pledge may rely on a sentimental subtext.

Such a sentimental subtext elides the difference between the masculine world of the public experience meeting and the private domestic realm of emotion and tender feelings. According to Hendler, "The drunkard's conversion, through tearful narration, into a sentimental, sympathetic, responsible man demonstrates that the boundaries between sentimentality as a characteristically feminine form of embodiment and publicly as a legitimating form of disinterested masculine abstraction were more porous than we usually assume" (127). The temperance pledge, then, seems to smooth out gender differences as it tenderizes men in sentimental bonds with men and women. Yet according to Gillian Silverman, sentimentalism is paradoxical: "Although it is predicated on shared feeling, sympathy can arise only in response to an initial disparity. . . . While it focuses on inherent equality and correspondence of feeling, it imagines these as consequences of fundamental asymmetries in the social order" (13). Sentimentality, then, contains a rhetoric of equality that actually disguises the way it sustains social difference. While on the one hand sentimentality promotes "a democratic world based in the communitarian values of common feeling, collective action, and public responsibility" (Silverman 5), it also "can imagine alignment of hearts only when it imagines disparity in circumstance" (ibid. 6).

If auditors are "bound" as witnesses by hearing a reformer's promise, are readers likewise "bound" in a contractual promise to what the author writes? In some ways we could assert that authors make a "contract" or "promise" with readers to tell a story or a coherent narration or argument. But is there reciprocity—does the reader promise anything to the text? In an ideal world, both reader and writer would engage in a promise to have faith in the written word to convey ideas. We don't think of such a contract as litigable, although with a receipt one can return a book to a store for a refund of money. Claybaugh reminds us that "social reform depended on print" (2), although there were other representations such as temperance parades and suffrage pageants. Likewise, the temperance pledge is a written document and the moment we as readers cast our eyes on the written document in a temperance story, we share the experience of reading along with the characters at the very moment they engage with the text. Most temperance stories with a redemptive denouement cannot end until the temperance pledge has been uttered or signed. As a performative utterance, then, the temperance pledge is vital to achieve narrative closure.

When drunkards sign the temperance pledge, their names become documented for all to witness, even when they leave the room. Their signature thus attests both to their recorded presence and to their anticipated absence. According to Derrida, "By definition, a written signature implies the actual or empirical nonpresence of the signer. But, it will be claimed, the signature also marks and retains his having-been present in a past *now* or present [*maintenant*] which will remain a future *now* or present [*maintenant*]" (*Limited Inc* 20). How does the signature reify the consent given in a promise? How do both a promise and a signature performatively act, whether written in a pledge or enacted by a slave who gives her word? The following chapter continues this exploration of promise and signature by focusing on Fanny Fern's novel *Ruth Hall*.

2

Theorizing the Signature in Fanny Fern's *Ruth Hall*

Performatively Speaking has been investigating the performativity of language uttered by characters in mid-nineteenth-century American fiction. This chapter will examine Fanny Fern's important 1854 novel *Ruth Hall* with an eye towards understanding the performativity of Ruth's signature, as well as of her printed name.[1] *Ruth Hall* explores the ways that Ruth becomes a businesswoman and a marketable commodity herself. Her entrance into the marketplace is made possible when she utters her name and pseudonym—Ruth's self-naming performs an action and enacts identity as well as litigable powers. The novel ends with an image of a bank stock, the only image in the book. The stock note and its legal language ("Be it known that Mrs. Ruth Hall," etc.) converts Ruth from an impoverished single mother to a successful businesswoman and stockholder. The stock in effect utters Ruth's name in such a way as to constitute an action that rearranges Ruth's relationship to capital and the market. I want to investigate what happens when Ruth deploys the pseudonym Floy, and the many questions it raises about signatures and utterances, authenticity, and the gendered nature of the iterability of her signature.

Ruth Hall depicts the social and economic rise of an impoverished but genteel widowed mother of two young girls to the rank of successful author. Based on the author's own life, the novel was excoriated by many when Fern's true identity was revealed to be that of Sara Payson Willis Eldredge, because the novel decries the poor treatment the author received from her brother and father, two well-known writers at the time. Fern's brother, Nathaniel Parker Willis, a vaunted literary figure, wrote prolifically and published important magazines, yet willfully refused to publish his sister's writings. N. P. Willis had helped the literary careers of other women such as Fanny Forrester and Grace Greenwood, but he felt too ashamed to let his colleagues know that a sister of his wrote anything so "vulgar" and "indecent" (Warren, introduction xiv). It was in his household that the fugitive slave Harriet Jacobs worked. I will return to this point later. Fern unflatteringly models Ruth's brother, the insensitive editor and snobby fop Hyacinth Ellet, on her own brother. Fern's father, Nathaniel Willis, also stood in the spotlight as an important man of letters; he published America's first religious newspaper, the *Recorder,* as well as the first newspaper for children, the *Youth's Companion,* and other periodicals. He also treated Fern with disdain and failed to support her and her children when she became a destitute widow. Fern did not just pillory her family in *Ruth Hall;* she likewise derides publishers who tried to take advantage of her. William Moulton, the publisher of the New York *True Flag,* recognized the unflattering portrayal of himself in *Ruth Hall* as the misogynist and conniving Mr. Tibbetts; to exact revenge, he revealed Fern's identity in print.

Readers rightly interpreted *Ruth Hall* as a novel of revenge because of the way Fern "outs" her neglectful relatives and publishers and portrays them as stingy, selfish, and small-minded. Although most reviews of the novel were positive, several reviewers specifically were horrified that a woman could so tarnish her male relatives' reputations. For example, a reviewer for the *New York Times* wrote in 1854, "If Fanny Fern were a man,—a man who believed that the gratification of revenge were a proper occupation for one who has been abused, and that those who have injured us are fair game, *Ruth Hall* would be a natural and excusable book. But we confess that we cannot understand how a delicate, suffering woman can hunt down even her persecutors so remorselessly. We cannot think so highly of [such] an author's womanly gentleness" (quoted in Warren, introduction ix). Clearly this reviewer was more shocked by Fern's gender rather than the fact that the novel airs out a family's dirty laundry. Moreover, since public reaction decried Fern personally, she brought further shame upon her relatives as readers assumed Fern was the type of woman who brings indecency upon herself (Warren, *Independent* 86).

To try to avoid this very censure and unwelcome intrusion into her privacy, Fern understandably published the novel under her pen name, a decision mirrored by the one facing her heroine. The author first began publishing under the pseudonym Fanny Fern in September 1851 and used the name as she began writing for different newspapers out of desperation to earn money to feed herself and her two daughters.[2] In 1852, Fern began writing a regular column for the New York *Musical World,* edited by her brother Richard Willis, which made her the first woman columnist in the

United States.[3] No one knew her true identity, but her published persona became one of the most popular names in America. In commenting on her fame, Fern said, "I think that when a lady has had a mud-scow and a hand-cart, a steamboat and a hotel, a perfume and a core of babies, not to mention tobacco and music, named for her; and when she is told what her name is, wherever she goes, till she is sick of the sound of it, that she does not earn for herself a boxed ear when she couples with her name the word 'famous'" (quoted in Warren, "Performative" 20). To capitalize on Fern's fame, the Auburn, New York, firm Derby and Miller published a book collection of her newspaper articles. By choosing royalty payments over a flat fee, Fern made almost $10,000 from the sales of *Fern Leaves from Fanny's Portfolio* (1853). By 1855, when Robert Bonner contracted her to write for the *New York Ledger* at $100 an article, Fern became the highest paid newspaper writer in the country. The name "Fanny Fern" was an institution, an income-generating identity, a branded product. Thus, in *Ruth Hall* when Fern theorizes Ruth's relationship to pseudonymity, identity, and naming, Fern also comments on her own past situation, poverty, vulnerability, the gendered nature of novelistic retribution, and the performativity of the signature.

The Signature Floy

To safeguard and ensure her claims to respectable womanhood, the heroine Ruth Hall needs to protect her anonymity, just as Sara Payson Willis Eldredge chose the pseudonym Fanny Fern. The nineteenth-century milieu closely associated a woman's dependence with her sexual purity; thus, an independent and financially savvy woman easily could be interpreted as dissolute and lacking in morals. Were a woman to sign her own name to a legal document, she would signal her independence to the world. But such independence would indicate an unprotected status and would leave her open and vulnerable to threats to her innocence and purity, the very qualities that could make her attractive to a middle-class husband (Weyler 111). In fact, as Karen Weyler points out, Ruth's search for newspaper employment as she wanders unaccompanied into male-dominated publishing offices to sell her skills sounds at times like prostitution. The novel also gestures towards prostitutes' boudoirs in Ruth's neighborhood, and Ruth herself shows sympathy for women who must sell themselves (ibid. 110).[4] To uncouple her virtue from her door-to-door selling of herself, Ruth relies on the benefit of a pen name.

The use of a pseudonym was also an established practice for many antebellum women writers because many considered it improper and unfeminine for a woman to express herself so publically in print. Mary Kelley discusses the way women writers could hide their skill or ambition behind the shelter of anonymity or a pseudonym: "At the very least, anonymity contributed to a sense of psychological security, and offered a partial, tenuous hold on social propriety. The literary domestics could write and, as it were, attempt to hide the deed" (125). Ruth's eventual success as a writer earns her money to support herself and her two young daughters, and she chooses to write under the pseudonymn Floy. We as readers do not see Ruth picking out a pen name or wrestling with options. We only find out her choice when Mr. Lescom of the *Standard* reads a letter from a fan who says that he will subscribe to the paper if Floy is to be a contributor. Mr. Lescom says parenthetically to Ruth, "a pretty *nom-de-plume* that of yours, Mrs. Hall" (130). Floy becomes a runaway sensation: readers do not know her identity as an actual living person, but Ruth's readers recognize Floy "as a voice for their own feelings of frustration and anxiety at the hands of a seemingly heartless and alienating public sphere" (Temple 151).

Gale Temple uses Walter Benjamin's theory of the bourgeois private sphere to analyze Ruth's (and other nineteenth-century women's) need to cleave a separation between her private identity and her public persona. Temple writes that privacy "depends upon the suppression of commercial as well as social interests in favor of the cultivation of a persona that will be observed, judged, and approved in the indeterminate future. The creation and cultivation of the interior (room, self) is always done with the public gaze in mind" (141). Although being in the public gaze threatened proper femininity, using a pen name did not always help women writers maintain a demur facade. According to Robert Gunn, since "the anonymity conferred by pseudonymity is not reducible to a form of privacy," then "paradoxically, pseudonymity . . . promotes the gaze as the governing protocol of public life even as it works to mitigate its effect" (27). The idea of fraught individualism, according to Temple, "connects femininity and gentility to a competitive ethic of market-oriented acquisitiveness that emphasizes proper forms of self-adornment" (136), which, especially for mid-nineteenth-century women, implied a link to commerce and consumerism. Discussing the gendered implications of becoming a published writer, Temple argues that "Ruth must first transcend the restrictions of poverty and gender in order to achieve social and economic success just as a man might. . . . *Ruth Hall* justifies and familiarizes the alienating and dehumanizing tendencies of the developing market, while it simultaneously sanctions and normalizes a virulently competitive individualism" (135). David Dowling, however, points out an opposite market tendency: Ruth was able to capitalize on the increasing demands for print material that encouraged publishers to seek out productive and popular women writers. Such changing market conditions broke down the prevailing separate spheres ideology as women became professional authors acknowledged by paid public labor (Dowling 347).[5] Ruth carefully tries to strike a balance between her capitalist self—the entrepreneurial, unladylike, business-oriented self that demands an assertion of the ego—and her recognition of the modest homebound woman that nonetheless increasingly began to enter a bottom-line-oriented enterprise premised on the currency of public name.[6]

Therefore, when Ruth attaches the name Floy to her published writings, she establishes a bourgeois separation between domesticity and marketplace. The pen name Floy creates and substantiates a partition between private self and public author where no such division existed before. The nom de plume calls a new identity into being and restructures Ruth's relationship to her readers and her legal status. Floy therefore performs an identity that reorganizes Ruth's class standing, relation to the market, and feminine consequence. I want to explore the ways Ruth's signing of Floy constitutes a performative utterance.

Jacques Derrida theorizes the link between naming and action when he writes about the U.S. Declaration of Independence. A phrase from the final paragraph of the Declaration reads, "We, therefore, the Representatives of the united States of America . . . by Authority of the good People of these Colonies, solemnly publish and declare, That these United Colonies are, and of Right ought to be Free and Independent States." Derrida discusses this sentence as an example of performative speech. As discussed earlier in this book, in his landmark *How to Do Things with Words,* J. L. Austin defines performative speech and elaborates on his claim that "the issuing of the utterance is the performing of an action" (6–7). As Benjamin Lee phrases it, "Performatives create the state of affairs that they appear to refer to" (66). Austin distinguishes between perlocutionary speech, which is speech that will lead to an action but is not the action itself, and illocutionary speech. An example of perlocutionary speech might be convincing or persuading someone to do something. Illocutionary speech, however, is the doing of an action in the moment of uttering it.

According to Derrida's example, when the Founding Fathers agreed on the wording that declared the colonies to be free and independent, they at that moment enacted what they uttered: they published and declared their freedom. Austin lays out several rules an utterance must follow in order to succeed or be felicitous, that is, in order for a performative utterance to achieve its intended force: the right words must be said in the right order at the right time in the right circumstances. Thus, the Founding Fathers understood the accepted conventional procedure of publishing and declaring and recognized the conventional effect it would have when King George III received the declaration. The Founding Fathers uttered the words in a conventional procedure under formal, recognized circumstances, and all in attendance understood that a new independent nation had been instantly created and substantiated. Further, according to Jason Frank, foundational documents actually create and substantiate the existence of a sovereign people as they assert their very authority; such texts "seek to elicit and enact the very people on whose authority their claims are made" (10). Ruth Hall similarly conjures her professional writerly identity in the moment of writing her authoritative signature. She creates the authority to which she appeals. Frank expresses this idea on a national scale: "The people of the American Revolution were not a unified identity awaiting expression but a virtual incipience awaiting enactment or dramatization. The people were enacted through the practical repertoires of the Revolution itself" (12).

The Founding Fathers legitimize and authorize (both in the sense of granting authority and of claiming authorship) when they sign their names to the bottom of the document. To what extent is the signature the authorizing utterance? Derrida questions whether the performative utterance itself enacts freedom, or whether the utterance reflects an already liberated nation. He asks, "Is it that the good people have already freed themselves in fact and are only stating the fact of this emancipation in [*par*] the Declaration? Or is it rather that they free themselves at the instant of and by [*par*] the signature of this Declaration?" ("Declaration" 9). This theory of the efficacy of the signature is extremely important for understanding Ruth Hall's rise from pauper to capitalist: the authority to declare oneself free or self-governing derives from the signatures at the bottom of the declaration. The "good people" of the united colonies affirm their potent and consequential words by affixing their names in another performative utterance that conforms to a conventional procedure in order to have an intended conventional effect.

Derrida complicates the idea of the self-sovereignty of the signature when he argues, "The signature invents the signer. This signer can only authorize him- or herself to sign once he or she has come to the end, if one can say this, of his or her own signature, in a sort of fabulous retroactivity. That first signature authorizes him or her to sign." Furthermore, he claims, "In signing, the people say . . . I have the right to sign, in truth I will already have had it since I was able to give it to myself. I will have given myself a name and an 'ability' or a 'power.' . . . A signature gives itself a name. It opens *for itself* a line of credit, *its* own credit, for itself *to* itself. The *self* surges up here in all cases (nominative, dative, accusative) as soon as a signature gives or extends credit to itself" ("Declaration" 10). To Derrida, the performative can create the conditions it needs in order to be effective. It alters, rather than being predicated upon, the context in which it is uttered. It establishes its own foundation, rather than being dependent upon a preexisting one.

According to this logic, the very act of Ruth signing her name to a contract ushers her empowerment or litigable entitlement into being. The mark of her signature performatively enacts authorization. As J. Hillis Miller argues, "A signature is clearly a speech act, as opposed to the constative answer to the question: 'What's your name?' A legal document such as a mortgage, a contract, or a marriage certificate is valid only when it is signed with a proper name, in the presence of witnesses. A check is an efficacious transfer of money only when it is signed by the right person" (119). However, Derrida's theory does not fully take into account the pressure of a gendered reading; his remarks about the performativity of the signature occlude gender differences in the implication of claiming the right to sign. In *Ruth Hall,* Fern seems acutely aware of Ruth's limited abilities to enter the marketplace, and thus the novel does a lot of work as it theorizes the gendered nature of the signature. If we submit Derrida's ideas to a gendered reading, we see that the act of Ruth signing her name demonstrates that all along Ruth, as a married woman, contained the right to herself; she extended to herself a line of credit that authorized her own abilities. By gifting herself a public writing persona and then signing that name, Ruth declares herself to be a self-governing woman author, able to enter into profitable legal contracts in the public marketplace. A woman's signature, therefore, can prove to be transgressive and liberating in a way that a man's cannot.

A dozen years earlier, Frederick Douglass also made this connection evident. In an effort to facilitate his escape from his master's Maryland plantation, Douglass forged a note of protection and signed it from his master. The note, which Douglass reprints in its entirety, reads:

> This is to certify that I, the undersigned, have given the bearer, my servant, full liberty to go to Baltimore, and spend the Easter holidays. Written with mine own hand, &c., 1835.
>
> WILLIAM HAMILTON,
> Near St. Michael's, in Talbot county, Maryland. (*Narrative* 99)

Douglass here impersonates his master and by signing the pass as his master literally authorizes himself: he becomes the author of the pass as he grants himself the authority and "full liberty" to travel to Baltimore. The phrase "written with mine own hand" is particularly poignant as it points to a situation of extreme irony: Douglass tells the truth that the pass was indeed written by his own hand, but he tells an untruth as he assumes a false identity. Douglass's writing under the name of William Hamilton differs from Ruth Hall writing under the name of Floy: Douglass steals the identity of his owner, whereas Ruth creates an identity that instantiates herself as self-owner. However, following Derrida, we can see that when Douglass signs the name of Hamilton, he performatively enacts his own authorization and grants himself the right to sign. He certifies that he, the very undersigned, has given the bearer, himself, his own full liberty to travel to Baltimore. Forging Hamilton's name opens "a line of credit" that grants and enacts credibility for Douglass.

Douglass's pass suggests the link between body and identity in that he crafts the pass to say "Written with mine own hand"; the legitimacy of the signature rests on it being forged by the selfsame hand and able to represent William Hamilton's presence in his absence (a concept that I will return to later in more detail). However, another signer in antebellum American literature concretizes this idea of embodied signature or utterance: Queequeg in Herman Melville's 1852 *Moby-Dick*. Queequeg must sign to join the crew of Captain Ahab's ship, the *Pequod,* as a harpooner.

Suspecting that Queequeg is illiterate, Peleg says, "Quohog there don't know how to write, does he? I say, Quohog, blast ye! dost thou sign thy name or make thy mark?" (85). Queequeg has sailed on Western whale-ships before and understands the convention of making a mark that encapsulates one's identity. Therefore, he take the pen and writes on the paper "a queer round figure which was tattooed upon his arm" (85). Quee-queg reifies body and identity by transferring a personal bodily marker to paper: he copies one of his tattoos onto the legal document. Interestingly, Melville records a picture in his manuscript, the only image to appear in the pages of the novel. This trope of bodily inscription continues in the novel, where Melville "explicitly links Queequeg's tattoo to writing and books by associating them with such terms as 'hieroglyphic mark,' 'writ-ten,' 'parchment,' 'treatise,' and 'volume'" (Rasmussen 128).

Multiplicity of Signatures

The previous section established that Ruth Hall needed to adopt a pseud-onym for her newspaper writing. But it is not clear to the *Pilgrim* publisher, Mr. Tibbets, why Ruth cannot use more than one singular pseudonym. To secure a more advantageous financial arrangement than the editor, at the *Standard*, Mr. Lescom, is willing to offer her, Ruth negotiates with Mr. Tibbets of the *Pilgrim*. At first Mr. Tibbets tries to lure Ruth away from her private publishing deal with the *Standard* by suggesting she avoid difficulties by writing under a second pen name: "'Well, if I conclude to engage you,' said Mr. Tibbets, 'I should prefer you would write for me over a different signature than the one by which your pieces are indicated at The Standard office, or you can write exclusively for my paper'" (132).

Ever the shrewd marketer, Ruth refuses to write under two different names because she understands the proliferation of her signature: "'With regard to your first proposal,' said Ruth, 'if I have gained any reputation by my first efforts, it appears to me that I should be foolish to throw it away by the adoption of another signature; and with regard to the last, I have no objection to writing exclusively for you, if you will make it worth my while" (ibid.). In other words, since Floy performs the alter-identity of a savvy, satirical, critical persona, Ruth does not want to dilute her powers by performing multiple identities under multiple signatures. She wants to consolidate her identity and earning powers by retaining a singular signature.

Ruth's understanding of the brand-recognition of a name is reflected in Fern's personal life: some readers asserted that Fern published under other names. To defend her position, in a letter dated 12 March 1853 to the editor of the *True Flag*, Fern wrote, "MR. EDITOR:—Will you oblige by saying to your readers that I never write for any publication over any other signature than that of FANNY FERN" (quoted in Homestead 218). The third newspaper to employ Fern, the *Musical World and Times*, recognized the power of her reputation, as it wrote on 10 December 1853, "The name of FANNY FERN alone commanded this unprecedented sale. What, then, is in a name? It would seem that there are a great many thousand dollars in *some* names" (ibid.). Fern understood that her name shaped readers' reception of a piece of literature: as Melissa J. Homestead argues, "The presence or absence of Fern's name alters the identity of the unchanged textual artifact, making it acceptable or unacceptable. . . . Her name, or lack thereof, thus powerfully shaped the circulation and reading of her texts" (221). Likewise, Ruth Hall acknowledges that her pen name Floy influences the circulation and reception of her newspaper columns and that she thus gains more credibility and recognition by sticking with one nom de plume. Homestead smartly discusses the ways that the vexing publishing industry, which reprinted Fern's pieces and attributed them variously, caused a multiplicity of identities. In contrast, we readers never actually get to see the articles that Ruth composes. We read *about* them and read her fans' adulation of her writing, but we never read firsthand what flows from Ruth's pen. Homestead points out that *Ruth Hall* "avoids confronting this authorial instability [i.e., the inability of readers to judge the quality of Ruth's writing] by obscuring it, by *not* representing Ruth's sketches. . . . We learn all about the *labor* of her writing, the scratching of her pen, her throbbing brow and weary fingers, and we know what she buys with her earnings ('bread for her children'); but the novel does not represent the object produced by that work" (226).

Ruth proves victorious in her desire to continue using the pseudonym Floy for more than one newspaper. However, she capitulates to lower remuneration than she would have liked. When Ruth declines Mr. Tibbet's offer to write under a different name, the paper makes her another offer "in which, since she would not consent to do otherwise, they agreed she should write over her old signature, 'Floy,' furnishing them with two articles a week" (132). While Ruth holds steadfast as a shrewd marketer of her unique product, publishers nonetheless still take advantage of her because she is perceived as a naive woman. Later, as her popularity rises, Ruth realizes that she is a valuable asset in demand by the newspapers and negotiates a higher salary. For the moment, however, "Ruth accepted the terms, poor as they were, because she could at present do no better, and because every pebble serves to swell the current" (132).

A flip side of the stability of a name is the capacity of another to undermine that very stability. The theme of instability of identity surfaces in *Ruth Hall:* Ruth is dismayed to find out that she cannot control reproduction of her sketches.[7] Mr. Tibbets, for example, threatens to issue a cheap edition of Ruth's collected articles (157). Homestead smartly calls attention to the juxtaposition of two letters Ruth receives, one from a fawning suitor and one from a book publisher. The two letters show the fluidity of identity Ruth must decide on and solidify: either she can "remarry and become little more than a high-class slave, or maintain economic independence and absolute self-possession through authorship" (222). Of course, Ruth chooses to reject the very marriage plot with which the novel opens, and instead favors financial self-sovereignty.

The concern in the novel with dilution of identity through unauthorized repetition of the signature corresponds to actual events in Fern's life. For example, many unknown writers piggybacked onto her success by fraudulently assuming her name. She humorously distanced herself from these usurpers by writing in the *True Flag* in 1853: "Never wrote one line of the above-named articles, which are traveling round the country, with a host of others like them. The way that illegitimate Ferns are smuggled into my well-regulated family, while my own mental children are kidnapped and baptized by aliens, is very curious to witness" (Warren, *Independent* 113). She satirically addressed these Fanny Fern imitators by advising them in 1853: "In choosing your signature, bear in mind that nothing goes down, now-a-days, but *alliteration.* For instance, Delia Daisy, Fanny Foxglove, Harriet Honeysuckle, Lily Laburnum, Paulena Poppy, Minnie Mignonette, Julia Jonquil, Seraphina Sunflower, etc" (ibid.). Later, another publishing firm fraudulently released a cookbook under the signature of Fanny Fern. Fern "realized the value of her name" and sued the firm in July 1856 to stop publication of the book that usurped her identity (Warren, introduction xix). She won both the case and the "exclusive right to the pseudonym's use" (ibid.). Further, she began to use the pen name in her personal life to such an extent that her friends, and even her husband, James Parton, began to call her Fanny, and she even signed some private letters under her assumed name (ibid.). Even her tombstone in Mount Auburn Cemetery in Cambridge, Massachusetts, reads "Fanny Fern."

Suitors' Signatures as Stable

While Ruth's signature proves to be falsifiable and reproducible unless legal action is taken to secure her copyright, the identity of her male suitors seems more stable and fixed. For example, since readers of Floy's columns closely identify the persona of Floy with an actual woman, many men fall in love with her and make her offers of marriage. As Homestead argues, "The more widely her sketches are reprinted, the more frequently strange men claim false alliances with her, making her look like a woman of easy virtue. Therefore, her popularity is inseparable from a chronic crisis of authorial reputation, the type of crisis to which Fern, as a 'lady,' is particularly susceptible" (213). Other men offer dubious business propositions. One admirer in particular writes a long, detailed letter that explains his scheme. He claims that his family "are and were highly respectable people" but have fallen on hard times, thus making his bid to go to college quite out of reach. He assumes Floy is rich and wants to strike a deal: "I don't ask you to lend me the money out of hand. What I propose is this: I will furnish you the subject for a splendid and thrilling story" (155). To buttress his claim to respectability, he writes, "My name, as you will see you when you come to my signature, is Reginald Danby" (154). This claim to respectability by signature stands in contrast to the "crisis of authorial reputation" faced by Ruth, especially in her identity as Floy. Danby understands that the gendered nature of his name suffices to carry credibility. His masculine signature represents a stable identity that does not erode despite his family's fall into impoverishment. Because of his gender, Danby confidently enters the marketplace of ideas and capital without worry about the damage or the multiplicity of his signature.

Nonpresence, Iterability

In further discussing the importance of the signature, Derrida argues that writing one's name comes to stand as a presence in the absence of the signer. Our unique and individual signature must be able to stand in proxy for us in different contexts. On the other hand, a signature is not unique because it must recognizably repeat again and again. J. Hillis

Miller writes, "A signature draws its force from the fact that it repeats earlier signatures by the same hand and can be checked against them for accuracy. In that sense, it is not unique at all" (44).

Derrida theorizes how the signature as a mark retains the "having-been present" of one who signed in the past and will retain its force into the future. The signature gestures towards a singular event in the past yet must remain identifiably reproducible in order to be effective in the future. When Ruth enters into the world of commerce, she enacts her signature to indicate her consent to the laws of publishing, contracts, copyright, and remuneration. Her signature is needed in order to complete a contractual agreement. Ruth is pleased when her publisher recognizes her self-sovereignty and needs to negotiate directly with her on a business level. For example, to finalize their agreement, John Walter of the *Household Messenger* needs Ruth to sign a contract. He sends her a letter that reads, "I enclose duplicates of a contract, which, if the terms suit you, you will please sign and return one copy *by the next mail;* the other you will keep" (146). The fact that Ruth can affix her signature to two copies and send one back to the publisher indicates the iterability of the signature. She will retain a copy and her signature will travel by mail and appear somewhere else as a representative of her consent.

According to Derrida, "For a writing to be a writing it must continue to 'act' and to be readable even when what is called the author of the writing no longer answers for what he has written, for what he seems to have signed, be it because of a temporary absence . . . [or] because he is dead." (*Limited Inc* 8). Ruth will continue to live after signing the contract, and her signature will continue to "act," even when she is miles away from her publisher. Her presence does not need to be immediate in order for her will to be enacted: "By definition, a written signature implies the actual or empirical nonpresence of the signer. But, it will be claimed, the signature also marks and retains his having-been present in a past *now* or present [*maintenant*] which will remain a future *now* or present [*maintenant*]" (ibid. 20). Thus, the very idea of the second contract being mailed back to the publisher requires Ruth's nonpresence. Yet her signature will carry its force and enable Mr. Walter to see Ruth's writings into print in his newspaper.

Fern's brother-in-law performatively uttered a disavowal of slander that he intended to act as his presence when, in January 1851, he wrote in a letter, "I deny ever having used the following words in regard to Mrs. S. P.

Farrington, my brother's wife 'That Mrs. S. P. Farrington, at other houses had received visitors, who remained all night, and supposed she did at the Marlboro.' I deny ever having uttered such words" (quoted in Warren, *Independent* 86). By writing "I deny," he engages in the performative act of denying. Similarly, Fern's second husband, Samuel P. Farrington, in an attempt to announce that he was no longer responsible for his wife's finances, placed a legal notice in the *Boston Daily Bee* in February of 1851 that stated, "I hereby forbid all persons harboring or trusting my wife, Sarah P. Farrington, on my account, from this date, having made suitable provision for her support" (ibid.). The written utterance "I hereby forbid" felicitously performs the act of forbidding. By appearing published in a legal document, the performative utterance stands in Farrington's absence and continues to exert a force in his absence. Fern continuously and permanently is forbidden from her ex-husband's financial support.

When Ruth signs her publishing contract, she enacts a litigable force. The act of signing legally binds her and her publisher in a mutual agreement enforceable by the powers of the state behind it. As a litigable entity, a signature works in the context of a history of laws. Laws themselves work because they cite convention: they refer to practices permitted and prohibited by communal agreement. According to Austin, as Miller paraphrases, a citation "is supposed to drag its original context implicitly along with it" (71). Miller argues that citing an utterance rather than performing it suspends its meaning (3). Because a signature accords with an accepted convention and has an accepted effect, it can be said to have "a sedimentation, a repetition that congeals, that gives the name its force" (Butler 36). Farrington's repetition in the above letter of the slander about Fern's supposed lack of virtue can be seen as both re-engaging the injurious language and as citing it. While uttering a denial of slander, he could take illicit pleasure in repeating the libel and thus rewounding. But if the denial cites his past utterance, the meaning becomes suspended and fails to injure.

According to Derrida, "In order to function, that is, to be readable, a signature must have a repeatable, iterable, imitable form; it must be able to be detached from the present and singular intention of its production" (*Limited Inc* 20). The fact of Ruth herself engaging in signing a contract suggests a context: a specific signer writing her signature and sending the resulting legal contract back to its designated publishing house recipient. In Austinian terms, such a written mark is iterable. Iterability is "the possibility for every mark to be repeated and still to function as a meaningful mark in new contexts that are cut off entirely from the original context" (Miller 78). James Loxley points out the seemingly inherent contradiction in the function of an iteration: "If a mark is iterable, it must be capable of occurring again, elsewhere, some other time: iterability allows the sameness of the mark only on the condition of this structural, internal difference. A mark, in other words, is therefore never quite identical to itself, never quite unified or entire of itself" (78). Iterability implies a severance from origin and the ability to sustain meaning even in new surroundings.

Yet because the signature, to be effective, must function in a variety of conditions, some of which may be wholly alien to the originary situation, including the absence of a recipient, the signature deconstructs Austin's supposition of a fixed and stable context. Derrida's most useful example of this property of a mark is his idea of the open nature of the post card. Anyone can cast his or her eyes onto a postcard's message; a postcard "falls into anyone's hands, a poor post card" (*Post Card* 51). Thus, the random reader of the postcard instantly becomes a recipient, however unintended. As Derrida writes, "the signers and the addressees are not always visibly and necessarily identical from one envoi to the other . . . [T]he signers are not inevitably to be confused with the senders, nor the addressees with the receivers, that is with the readers (*you* for example)" (ibid. 5). Eventually, for Derrida, language itself is a like a post card: it is both public and private and liable to be misread or to arrive at the wrong destination.

Bank Stock

The final aspect of the performativity of the signature that *Ruth Hall* explores is the reproduction of Ruth's name on a bank stock. The only image, the only illustration, to appear in the text is that of a bank stock in the penultimate chapter. Fern enacts what Julie Nelson Christoph terms a "strategy of placement": "a rhetorical choice in relation to the material constraints of a writer's physical space and geography, as well as to placement within ideological debates" (669). The publisher Mr. Walter addresses Ruth as Floy and tells her, "I have obeyed your directions, and here is something you may well be proud of," and hands Ruth a piece of paper. We as readers then see the actual piece of paper Mr. Walter hands Ruth. The text breaks from its conventional format in order to reproduce an image of a fancy document that reads, "Be it known that Mrs. Ruth Hall, of _____, is entitled to one hundred shares of the Capital Stock of the Seton Bank, and holds the same subject to the conditions and stipulations contained in the Articles of Association of such Institution; which shares are transferable on the Books of the Association by the said Mrs. Ruth Hall or her Attorney, on surrender of this Certificate" (209). Ruth's reaction to becoming a stockholder is never shown—the novel then switches perspective and shows us Mr. Walter and Ruth's daughter Nettie sharing laughter and excitement at Ruth's newfound success. The image of the bank stock emphasizes the immediacy of the moment: we as readers serve as witnesses to Ruth's success as we read the bank stock along with her.

The picture of the bank stock, then, is tangible evidence of Ruth's achievement. It stands by itself as a pictorial summary of her aspirations and accomplishment, as if Ruth does not need to comment. Yet although it is an image, it still contains words. The legal wording, "Be it known that Mrs. Ruth Hall," is performative—it enacts the condition of making the knowledge known, and of entering Ruth into a legally binding contract with the Seton Bank. At the same time, it reconstitutes Ruth's relationship to the market and casts her as an investor and stockholder in the world of financial transactions. The utterance of Ruth's name in the context of the stock performs an identity anew, one that she did not hold a few moments before.

Derrida reminds us that the efficacy of Ruth's name depends on the integrity of a law-abiding state government with effective powers. In a lawless society, the meaning of contracts dissolves as unenforceable. "The constitution and the laws of your country somehow guarantee the signature, as they guarantee your passport and the circulation of subjects and of seals foreign to this country, of letters, of promises, of marriages, of checks" ("Declaration" 11). In order for Ruth's name to felicitously perform its identity, there must be a state-supported framework to protect and sanction a legal relationship. Ruth's name on a stock certificate, therefore, co-opts Ruth into structures of authority and recognition.

However, Mr. Walter purchases the stock on Ruth's behalf. The bank stock acts as a third-party utterance that transforms Ruth's status and entry into the marketplace. It is not Ruth who utters her identity, as she does when she signs a contract or signs her name to a newspaper column. Ruth's contractual signature and her name on the bank stock stand as different performative utterances, yet both conjure the same litigable identity. As a third-person running comment on Ruth, the stock acts as a sort of Bakhtinian skaz, which Jennifer Harris defines as "written speech fashioned to represent oral patterns revealing socially distinct points of view" (616). Cast in official legalistic performative language, the bank stock represents a very distinct point of view from the condition of impoverished widowhood that Ruth had been living in and laboring under. Thus, as a different representation of speech, the stock performatively utters a new situation.

Maria C. Sanchez points out the irony of Ruth's name appearing in print on a commodity-oriented piece of paper. According to Sanchez, the "structure of mid-nineteenth-century law (coverture) ensured that although it was the death of Ruth's husband which precipitated her poverty, it was only as a widow that Ruth could have acceded to such a public transaction. Unless widowed, the coexistence of a white woman's name and the feminine married title on a public documentation of property represented an uncommon event" (48). Harris makes the link between money and self-sovereignty concrete when she argues, "Capital and the ability to speak on one's own behalf and be heard are inextricable in the text" (349–50). While the bank stock utters Ruth's name, it can only do so if she is vulnerable and not protected by a man. Joyce Warren points out, however, that in some states a married woman could own stock without necessarily being a widow. The law differed from state to state, but Massachusetts passed a law in 1845 that allowed a married woman to hold personal property apart from her husband. In most instances, the law applied to personal property that a wife brought with her to the marriage or that she inherited or received as a gift. Since the law did not yet cover a married woman's access to her own earnings, it would be unlikely that that she would have enough money to actually purchase stock, but she could own it. Mr. Walter purchases stock for Ruth with Ruth's earned income. A man purchasing stock on her behalf at once exposes her defenseless widowed status and yet acknowledges her legal right to defend herself by being co-opted into capitalist investing.

Both Sanchez and Lauren Berlant also point out the irony of Ruth's name appearing printed on a legal transaction: at the time, it was more common for black women's names to appear in print, particularly on bills of sale or offers for capture and return. A stock stands in relation to ownership, a status from which slave women were alienated. Sanchez writes that, the "fact that in 1854, black women's names continuously appeared on public documents as possessions in and of (but not for) themselves lends the bank note its extraordinary nature; to own bank stock a woman must own, at the very least, her own self, and thus the bank note serves as a kind of self-title" (48). Berlant reads the ending of *Ruth Hall* against the ending of *Incidents in the Life of a Slave Girl* by Harriet Jacobs, a slave who worked in the household of Fern's brother N. P. Willis. Jacobs also meditates on the wording of a document fundamental to her identity: her bill of sale. Jacobs, upon being told that Mrs. Bruce purchased her freedom and holds the bill of sale, writes, "'The bill of sale!' Those words struck me like a blow. So I was *sold* at last! A human being *sold* in the free city of New York! The bill of sale is on record, and future generations will learn from it that women were articles of traffic in New York, late in the nineteenth century of the Christian religion" (200). While both Ruth Hall and Harriet Jacobs end their narratives with their names printed on official documents, the women's standing in relation to self-ownership could not be more distant. As Berlant comments, "Both women have struggled to procure these papers, but while the one denotes the minimal unit of freedom experienced by an American citizen, the other denotes a successful negotiation of the national-capitalist public sphere, a profitable commodification of female pain and heroism in an emerging industry of female cultural workers" (448).

According to Austin, speech act theory violates the traditional philosophical assumption that to say something "is always and simply to *state* something" (12). As we have seen in the case of the signature and the bank stock, those words are not simply facts that can be true or false, but utterances that do something as they say it. The utterances succeed felicitously because they are uttered in a mutually agreed-upon world of words where such utterances effect action. Fanny Fern, an astute writer who crafts her words carefully, seems aware of the performativity of the ways in which Ruth gets co-opted into capitalism and self-sovereignty. As *Ruth Hall* demonstrates, a woman can performatively utter herself into the business world of transaction and success.

3

The Scarlet *A* as Action

Ruth Hall needed to sign contracts with her publisher in order to guarantee receipt of payments and to clarify her obligation to the newspapers. Too much was at stake for both Ruth and her publisher—reputation, exclusivity, financial security—to rely on a verbal agreement or a cheerful handshake. Although Ruth promises to write regularly for the *Household Messenger* and Mr. Walter promises to pay her, without a written agreement between the two parties Ruth could balk on her writing obligations or the newspaper could stall on its remittances to her. Ruth's signature, then, spoke her consent to the terms of a publishing contract. The repetition of writing the letters of her name performed the act of reifying her presence and inaugurated her position as a player in the world of market-based transactions. Her name needed to be spelled correctly to validate her legal standing; otherwise the performative act would fail. But what about the writing of an individual letter? Can a single letter, rather than a whole name, also effectively act?

If in Nathaniel Hawthorne's *The Scarlet Letter,* Puritan society views Hester Prynne and her scarlet letter as "a living sermon" (46) and "the text of the discourse" (59), how does Hester's scarlet badge articulate such a sermon or text? When Roger Chillingworth tells Hester that the town magistrates discussed the possibility of allowing her to remove the scarlet letter, Hester replies that were she worthy of dispensing with the letter, "it would fall away of its own nature, or be transformed into something that should *speak* a different purport" (110, emphasis added). Examining Hester's scarlet utterances ("a living sermon" and "the text of the discourse" that can "speak a . . . purport") as performative speech acts, rather than as constative statements about Hester's moral or spiritual situation, raises many questions about the performativity of language in Hawthorne's novel and how to do things with a letter.

For over 150 years readers have understood the *A* as serving as a confession. Viewing the *A* through the lens of performative speech theory, however, allows us to see that Hester's single-letter utterance simultaneously performs both state-sponsored injurious language and also performative dissent that by necessity cites or repeats the very injury. Hester's social position in Puritan Boston demonstrates that language has agency and that Hester, as an object of language's "injurious trajectory" (Butler 1), has been hurt by speech. Hawthorne summarizes this duality between the *A* speaking its force as a juridical, enforced confession of guilt, and also as a reaffirming, rebellious confession, in chapter 5 when he writes, "The very law that condemned her—a giant of stern features, but with vigor to support, as well as to annihilate, in his iron arm—had held her up, through the terrible ordeal of her ignominy" (55). When Hester wears the scarlet *A* she articulates punitive, official, regulatory language, and yet, as her elaborate embroidery of the *A* indicates, she simultaneously registers a resistance that constitutes and inaugurates identity.

This call and response nature of injurious language and performative dissent proves to be part of the very framework of *The Scarlet Letter,* as structural as the omnipresent scaffold. As performative speech, the letter *A* both complies with and resists convention and thereby variously affects the utterer and the receiver. But if the scarlet *A* is speech because it "speaks" one purport or another, what does it say? If it is an act, what does it do?[1] Considering the scarlet letter as a speech act shifts the reader's focus from viewing the *A* as a constative statement about morality to viewing the *A* as the doing of an action. What exactly this action comprises becomes quite complicated since, following Jacques Derrida, each performative act creates its own context and contains referents already embedded in it.[2] We must also keep in mind who speaks the sartorial ornament—Hester herself as she wears it, or the governing Puritan officials through her—for Hester simultaneously corporeally embodies the utterance and seems to serve as a mouthpiece for the magistrates.

This chapter aims to show that the *A* can simultaneously "speak the purport" of both injurious litigious language and performative dissent. To make this argument, I will draw upon theories of pornographic speech and hate speech. I will consider the scarlet letter itself as sexualized speech and as a citation. By recognizing that the illocutionary force of language depends on context and convention, we will see that Pearl's green seaweed

A and Dimmesdale's deathbed self-flagellation fail as felicitous speech acts. I will argue that Hester's artistic gold-threaded embroidery of the *A* mimics the magistrates' official speech by framing their linguistic sentencing. However, Hester's riff on their punishment reclaims their injurious language, cites it, and reassigns its authority. I intend to show that Hawthorne stages a theory of the performativity of language, in language itself, at the level of the most basic utterance—a single letter.

It is important first to identify some places in the novel where Hawthorne shows he clearly understands the performative power of speech. When the Puritan magistrates legislate that Hester must wear the scarlet letter as punishment, they reify the link between speech and action by enfranchising a linguistic utterance to carry the force of an act. The Puritan magistrates choose to castigate Hester first by imprisoning her, then by sentencing her to wear a textual confession of her sin for three hours on a pillory, and finally by compelling her to wear the insignia of disgrace for the rest of her life. The magistrates clearly intend the *A* to mark Hester bodily: "Woman, it is thy badge of shame!" (75). Franny Nudelman explains that by "placing the A on Hester's breast, the Puritan fathers expose Hester's sin and hope that the humiliation she suffers will subdue her rebellious spirit" (200).

Hawthorne further uncoils the performative action of speech in the townspeople's reactions. For example, determined to discover Hester's partner in sin, a voice from the crowd gathered around the scaffold demands, "Speak, woman! . . . Speak; and give your child a father!" (50). This angry order is premised on the assumption that Hester's uttering the name of Pearl's father will do more than reveal the baby's paternity: her utterance, her pronouncing his name, will conjure his identity into being and thereby create, substantiate, and reify a father where none had existed before.[3] Her potential speech act would not only name a man but would perform the action of generating a father. In her stubborn rebuff, Hester retorts, "I will not speak! . . . And my child must seek a heavenly Father; she shall never know an earthly one!" (50), thus clinching for readers the connection between speech and action. In another example of performative speech, while at the brook side Hester strips off the *A* and exclaims, "See! With this symbol I undo it all" (130), thus uttering a performative ("I undo") that acts to stop further scarlet utterances.

Even from the novel's preface, "The Custom-House," the scarlet letter has a force. Hawthorne describes the ragged scarlet *A* he finds among

Surveyor Pue's papers as imbued with "deep meaning in it, most worthy of interpretation," that "streamed forth from the mystic symbol, subtly communicating itself to my sensibilities, but evading the analysis of my mind" (26).[4] Having placed the letter on his breast, Hawthorne's narrator "experience[s] a sensation not altogether physical, yet almost so, as of burning heat; and as if the letter were not of red cloth, but red-hot iron" (25). In this description, the letter *A* burns; it produces a feeling understood as physical pain. The burning sensation causes the narrator to shudder and to "involuntarily let it fall upon the floor" (ibid.). Later, the narrator will report that the letter "burned on Hester's bosom" (111). Clearly, the letter *A* here carries a certain force: it acts upon the world with its burning action. Yet the letter nonetheless "evades" analysis. The evasion of meaning, then, lies not in the letter's fiery physical property, but in its multiple interpretive possibilities.

As discussed earlier, in his landmark *How to Do Things with Words*, J. L. Austin defines performative speech and explains that "the issuing of the utterance is the performing of an action" (6–7) and that "*by* saying or *in* saying something we are doing something" (12). Elin Diamond explicates Austin by writing that a performative utterance "does not refer to an extra-linguistic reality but rather enacts or produces that to which it refers" (4). Austin further lays out several rules an utterance must follow in order to succeed or be felicitous; that is, in order for a performative utterance to achieve its intended force. It is worth recalling that for a speech act to have potency, "there must exist an accepted conventional procedure having a certain conventional effect, that procedure to include the uttering of certain words by certain persons in certain circumstances" (Austin 14).

The scarlet letter performs what Austin would call a verdictive illocution; that is, the *A* authoritatively renders a ruling. Austin explains that, "As official acts, a judge's ruling makes laws; a jury's finding makes a convicted felon; an umpire's giving the batsman out, or calling a fault or a no-ball, makes the batsman out, the service a fault, or the ball a no-ball" (154). In other words, an umpire's authoritative standing endows his speech with a force unattainable to an observer or anyone who is understood by society *not* to hold such a rank.[5] Thus, as a punitive measure imposed by the Puritan magistrates, the scarlet *A* enacts the verdictive of guilt and sin.

As the magistrates' speech, the scarlet letter also performs an exercitive force, which Austin defines as the "giving of a decision in favour of or against a certain course of action, or advocacy of it. It is a decision that

something is to be so, as distinct from a judgment that it is so; it is advocacy that it should be so, as opposed to an estimate that it is so; it is an
award as opposed to an assessment; it is a sentence as opposed to a verdict.
. . . Its consequences may be that others are 'compelled' or 'allowed' or 'not
allowed' to do certain acts" (155). As an example of an exercitive illocution,
Rae Langton argues that "the speech acts of apartheid that legitimate dis-
criminatory behavior and unjustly deprive blacks of certain rights have an
exercitive force that would be absent if they were made by speakers who
did not have the appropriate authority" (304). Thus, similar to the former
South African apartheid government, the Puritan magistrates perform an
excercitive illocution via the scarlet letter because the *A* legitimates discrimination and isolation and authorizes Hester's social ostracism.

For example, Hawthorne describes the force of the *A* when he writes,
"The effect of the symbol—or rather, of the position in respect to society
that was indicated by it—on the mind of Hester Prynne to herself, was
powerful and peculiar" (106–7). Further, "Every gesture, every word, and
even the silence of those with whom she came in contact, implied, and
often expressed, that she was banished, and as much alone as if she inhab-
ited another sphere" (58). In addition, children fear Hester and "when
strangers looked curiously at the scarlet letter,—and none ever failed to do
so,—they branded it afresh into Hester's soul" (59). The scarlet letter keeps
Hester detached, enabling her to sense "hidden sin" (60) in others: "Sometimes, the red infamy upon her breast would give a sympathetic throb,
as she passed near a venerable minister or magistrate" (61). Sometimes
a young maiden would blush upon viewing the *A,* "as if her purity were
somewhat sullied by that momentary glance" (60), thus further marking
Hester as inferior.

From the opening chapter, the magistrates employ language to deprive
Hester of a normative civil status and relegate her to an inferior position
in society. Many readers of the novel would concur with Richard Brodhead that the Puritan magistrates utter Hester's *A* as she wears it: "The A
becomes the Puritans' A, the emblem through which they impose their
judgment on a violator of their communal values" ("Method" 397). As
a psychological punishment, not a corporal one,[6] it is the magistrates' *A*
itself that exerts a force on the community and transforms Hester into a
"living sermon" (46) and "the text of the discourse" (59). The *A* can do this
because the Puritan magistrates have "the *juridical* power to inflict pain
through language" as representatives of the state that "retains the power

to create and maintain certain forms of injurious speech" (Butler 48, 101). The magistrates use speech performatively to produce a punishing, disciplinary injury. Following Langton's claim that "to subordinate someone is to put them in a position of inferiority or loss of power, or to demean or denigrate them" (303), the magistrates' authority renders the *A* as injurious language that subordinates and silences Hester. Because "powerful people can generally do more, say more, and have their speech count for more than can the powerless" (Langton 299), the Puritan magistrates' scarlet utterance subordinates Hester and prevents her from engaging in society as other citizens do. As an illocutionary act of subordination, the magistrates' *A* "determine[s] civil status" (Langton 302) because the letter *A*, as an utterance, immediately creates and substantiates a social framework that places Hester in a disadvantageous position within a "structural relation of dominance" (Butler 18) relative both to the Puritan magistrates who have sentenced her and to the townspeople who ostracize her.

This "structural relation of dominance" applies to theories of both hate speech and pornography. Although the Boston magistrates do not hold feelings of odium against Hester, hate speech, according to Butler, "constitutes its addressee at the moment of its utterance" (ibid.). She goes on to argue that "it does not describe an injury or produce one as a consequence; it is, in the very speaking of such speech, the performance of the injury itself, where the injury is understood as social subordination" (ibid.). Racial slurs and other hateful words work their effect by placing the addressee in a socially subordinated position. For example, about the word *nigger,* Randall Kennedy writes that the hateful slur "lay at the core of a recollection that revealed to me the pain my mother continues to feel on account of wounds inflicted upon her by racists during the era of Jim Crow segregation" (xii). Toni Morrison makes a similar claim when she asserts that oppressive language "does more than represent violence; it is violence."

Butler and Morrison concur that injurious language is itself the action, not a verbal comment that consequently produces harm. Like hate speech, the legal directive that Hester must wear language as a badge of shame constitutes Hester as a civil inferior. The *A* performatively speaks subordination and instantiates a structural relation of dominance that places Hester at the bottom of the hierarchy. The letter *A* thus constructs Hester, in Butler's words, "unilaterally, exhaustively" (68): it reinforces a certain social structure that marks Hester differently and separates her from her peers. From the array of castigatory choices available, the magistrates have chosen language to be the most appropriate. Constituted discursively through the letter *A*, Hester foresees that wearing the letter will turn her into a collective figure of sin, forcing her to surrender her individuality and instead "become the general symbol at which the preacher and moralist might point, and in which they might vivify and embody their images of woman's frailty and sinful passion" (55). Thus, Hawthorne's readers witness language as an act or an action that injures.

The social structure of dominance established by hate speech operates by using words with an embedded history. Hate speech achieves its force by operating on the principle that a particular slur conjures a specific historical reference that constitutes its subject in a hurtful position. Hurling a word that has no history or meaning is not injurious language. As Butler points out, "The speaker who utters the racial slur is thus citing that slur, making linguistic community with a history of speakers" (52). The Puritan magistrates, in choosing the letter *A* as punishment, draw upon the fact that the letter *A* has an embedded history within the community as part of one common punishment for adultery. Were Hester to wear another symbol, say, a circle or even a different letter of the alphabet, she would not feel the burn of subordination or ostracism. In other words, the shape of the letter, and its embedded historical precedence, level damage. Because of its entrenched status among the New Englanders, the letter *A* "speaks its purport effectively," or, as Austin would term it, felicitously.

Arguments about pornographic speech support the contention that like pornography, the *A* enacts subordinating speech that "determines women's inferior social status" (Langton 297). Pornography is "something that ranks [women], judges them, denigrates them, and legitimates ways of behaving that hurt [them]" (ibid. 311). If the magistrates' imposing the sartorial punishment on Hester is coercive and authoritative, it sets the standards by which language can be used and determines that the *A* enacts a lower social standing among the Puritans. The authority of pornography "discredits women's dissent" (McGowan 30) and "silences the speech of women" by placing "structural constraints on women's speech" (Langton 322, 323). Because the scarlet letter has the "authority of a monopoly" on language (ibid. 312), it stands as an illocutionary utterance with a perlocutionary effect on the townspeople: they believe Hester to be guilty and believe discrimination against her to be legitimate. The ignominy and inferiority induced by the scarlet letter, for example, threatens the magistrates' confidence in Hester's ability to rear her daughter: "It is because of the stain which that letter indicates, that we would transfer thy child to other hands" (76). Although by this power of speech, the *A* subordinates, I will later demonstrate how Hester resists the silencing, monopolizing effect of the authority's language.

Since the Puritan juridical power is male, one could extend arguments about pornography to claim that the scarlet letter holds performative functions by "encoding the will of a masculine authority, and compelling a compliance with its command" (Butler 67). The letter *A* thus constitutes a "sexualization of speech" (Butler 76) because it articulates Hester's bodily desires, her erotic nature, and her sexual deviancy. As sex-based discrimination, the scarlet letter utters Hester's transgression and attempts to regulate and punish female sexuality. For example, the *A* evidences Hester's extra-marital sexual activity and thereby disqualifies her from sewing wedding veils for brides. The letter *A* enacts a "carrier function" that deems illicit female sexuality to be contagious and susceptible to transmissibility (Butler 115). Nudelman writes that "Hawthorne ties [Hester's] criminal identity, and the course of her punishment, to a rhetoric of maternity" (195). The magistrates' sexualized speech "creates the grounds that justify it[self]" (Miller 27), and thus further subordinates and marginalizes Hester by deeming the male monopoly of language to be the tabula rasa upon which Hester can be inscribed.

Yet at the same time, the *A* unsexes Hester so that her feminine attractiveness and softness wither. When she wears the *A,* Hester keeps her hair tied up. At the brook side when she tears off the letter and lets her hair down, "her sex, her youth, and the whole richness of her beauty, [come] back from what men call the irrevocable past" (138). After Pearl, the living analog of the scarlet letter, insists that her mother wear her customary token, Hester refastens the *A* and "next gather[s] up the heavy tresses of her hair, and confine[s] them beneath her cap. As if there were a withering spell in the sad letter, her beauty, the warmth and richness of her womanhood, depart[], like fading sunshine; and a gray shadow seem[s] to fall across her" (143). The letter *A* hereby commands a masculinized regulation of language. As the magistrates' sexualized speech it simultaneously articulates female adultery and marks Hester as sexually fallen.

By becoming the magistrates' exemplary "living sermon" and "text of the discourse," Hester textualizes female sexuality. The alphabetic sign, as an emblem of language, refers specifically to Hester's eroticism. According to Patricia Crain, when the letter is tethered to the adulteress, "the two exchange some qualities: the alphabet becomes sexualized while the woman is alphabetized" (196). Crain points out that in sentimental fiction, the figure of the mother is usually desexualized. However, in this novel, the *A* both desexualizes Hester and yet marks her as sexually guilty. Crain argues that "in Hawthorne's fictive world, the sign melds with the person. In a kind of homeopathic therapy, the state's alphabetizing of Hester resexualizes the maternal body even as it attempts to desexualize it" (196).

The scarlet letter's ability to perform such regulatory structures of power depends entirely on context. Much intellectual work has been done on the importance of context to an utterance's efficaciousness or felicity, with Austin laying the groundwork and Derrida finding fissures in it. Sandy Petrey states that "language's communal power is the effect of its 'performative' capacity" (3). The key word here for an utterance to perform successfully is "communal," or as Petrey says, "collective acceptance" and "collective accord" (5). By bodily uttering the magistrates' *A,* Hester follows the accepted communal convention of wearing a letter as a mark of criminality to achieve the conventional punitive effect of confessing a moral wrong. All of the townspeople recognize, comprehend, and mutually enforce the meaning of the infamous badge.

For example, at our first glance of Hester wearing the scarlet *A,* the narrator informs us that the letter's "wild and picturesque peculiarity" nonetheless "transfigured" Hester since it seems to have the "effect of a spell, taking her out of the ordinary relations with humanity, and inclosing her in a sphere by herself" (41). When Hester steps forward out of the town jail in the novel's second chapter, the reader finds a virtual Greek chorus of commentators ready to let readers know how Hester would appear to "a sensitive observer" (40). A female spectator derides the way Hester has made "a pride out of what they, worthy gentlemen, meant for a punishment" (41). A "gossip" praises Hester's needlework skills; another sneers that our heroine's "rich gown" should be replaced with "a rag of mine"; a third reprimands her gossiping companions by saying that "not a stitch in that embroidered letter, but she has felt it in her heart" (ibid.).

When Hester ascends the scaffold carrying the infant Pearl, the narrator asserts that a Roman Catholic among the Puritans would be reminded of "the image of Divine Maternity" (42). Most significantly, the Puritan magistrates pronounce Hester "the figure, the body, the reality of sin" (55), a designation that takes effect only when she dons the scarlet letter. Sacvan Bercovitch points out that "the novel begins with an act of interpretation, or rather with a series of interpretations. Neither Hester nor Dimmesdale nor Pearl is the novel's interpretive hero; the Puritan community is" (47). These comments by Hester's fellow Puritans are important to stress because they demonstrate the authoritative and collective act of subordination enacted by the scarlet utterance. The comments provide meaning and relevance because the town folk constitute an interpretive community that provides a context in which the *A* can have force.

Derrida, however, undermines theories about the necessity of convention and context by claiming that a mark can still have its force in the absence of a sender or receiver (Miller 91–92). A mark can function, Derrida claims, in the absence of a receiver, thus deconstructing Austin's supposition of a stable context. Derrida's most useful example of this property of a mark is his idea of the open nature of the post card, which I discussed in the previous chapter. Derrida argues that any random reader instantly becomes a recipient, however unintended (*Postcard* 5). Therefore, according to Derrida, the postcard creates its own recipients and new context. Or, as Miller phrases it, "a performative utterance creates the conventions it needs in order to be efficacious, rather than depending on their prior existence for its felicity" (Miller 112).

According to Austin, an utterance may oscillate between being performative or constative. We do see in *The Scarlet Letter* that the *A* can fluctuate in an Austinian sense between being read as a comment on Hester's moral worth and as performative utterance. But Derrida finds the undecidability of a locution's status as constative or performative to be essential to meaning. Undecidability, far from detracting from an utterance's force, commands its felicity. Undecidability is necessary "because for an ungrounded or self-grounding performative to work, it must convey the illusion, fable, or fiction of having a solid, preexisting ground or law to erect itself on, while claiming for itself autonomous performative force. . . . The text needs both possibilities in order to bring about what it names" (Miller 127).

Hawthorne seems to understand these points about context and undecidability in speech act theory, for he plays with the felicitous potential of Hester's performative utterance. He shows us, for example, that Native Americans and sailors, not part of Boston's conventional procedures or communal life, remain immune to the letter's intended effect. As Hester walks through town, the Indians "fastened their snake-like black eyes on Hester's bosom; conceiving, perhaps, that the wearer of this brilliantly embroidered badge must needs be a personage of high dignity among her people" (156). The mariners, "learning the purport" of the letter, stare at Hester in the marketplace as if "fixed there by the centrifugal force of the repugnance which the mystic symbol inspired" (ibid.). The Indians' and sailors' different interpretations of the letter supports Miller's claim about context: "When a sentence or other mark is reused in a different context, it does not remain the same. It is altered" (81). In the context of Derridean unintended readers, the letter A does not perform its force; it fails to act performatively as an act of subordination. Since the Indians and sailors do not form part of the collective that endows the A with the right condition, Hawthorne writes, "The letter was the symbol of her calling. Such helpfulness was found in her,—so much power to do, and power to sympathize,—that many people refused to interpret the scarlet A by its original signification. They said that it meant Able; so strong was Hester Prynne, with a woman's strength" (106). As outsiders to the Puritan community, the Indians and sailors interpret the A very differently.

So far I have been examining the scarlet letter as injurious speech authorized and legitimated by the Puritan magistrates and vocalized corporeally, or ventriloquially, on Hester's breast. Yet we must also consider the scarlet letter as being uttered simultaneously by Hester herself. Were she to wear the A as a sincere admission of sin, the letter would enact a force through the convention of confession. In Hawthorne's novel, the Puritans are "a people amongst whom religion and law were almost identical" (37), and thus for whom confession carried social and religious import. Ernest Baughman identifies public confession as customary in Puritan society and claims that confession had both a spiritual and legal basis (207), thereby rendering it part of Puritan society's conventions.[7] For an utterance to succeed felicitously, Austin theorizes that the utterance must be stated with intention and sincerity (15). If someone makes the illocutionary utterance "I confess that . . ." but does not truthfully confess a sin, then the utterance is infelicitous. To succeed, therefore, the utterance must be an "outward and visible sign" of an "inward and spiritual act" (ibid. 9).

According to the Puritans, a minister cannot grant absolution unilaterally; the sinner must do the confessing by verbally externalizing his or her sin. For example, Roger Chillingworth believes it is salutary to clear one's conscience through confession because unconfessed sin can manifest itself in signs, as with the unmarked grave he mentions that is symbolically clogged with weeds: "[the weeds] grew out of [the dead man's] heart, and typify, it may be, some hideous secret that was buried with him, and which he had done better to confess during his lifetime" (87). Reverend Wilson also understands the confessional power of the *A*, for he believes that it wrongs woman's nature to "force her to lay open her heart's secrets in such broad daylight" (48). Yet he also distinguishes between Hester's sin and her forced confession of it, conceding that "the shame lay in the commission of the sin, and not in the showing of it forth" (48). We never hear Hester orally confess to a sin, but she admits the scarlet letter compels a pedagogical lesson: she claims that "this badge hath taught me,—it daily teaches me,—it is teaching me at this moment,—lessons whereof my child may be the wiser and better" (75). Brodhead argues that the scarlet *A* "begins its life as an instrument of civil punishment—one of those visible markings that Foucault finds characteristic of pre-modern punishment, where punishment takes the form of publicly inscribing the power of the state on the body of the offender" (189). Thus, Puritan society sees the scarlet accessory as an exterior sign of Hester's interior condition.

Because Hester admits that her punishment teaches her to be a better mother, it does seem as if Hester at times sincerely utters the magistrates' letter *A*. But we must consider whether the Puritan magistrates and Hester say the same thing when they both utter the scarlet letter. In the case of the former, the *A* constitutes state-sanctioned speech. Yet Hester appropriates the performative for her own use through her elaborate embroidery. Because Hester does not have state-backed power in her scarlet utterance, the difference between the magistrates as speakers of the *A* and Hester as the speaker of the *A* must be examined.

As a skilled needlewoman, Hester alters the convention of her punishment through her artistry, which upsets the accepted punitive convention yet still draws upon a communal recognition of the *A* being intact. The narrator comments that the letter's finery is "greatly beyond what was allowed by the sumptuary regulations of the colony." Hawthorne reveals the meaning of the letter to be indeterminate and mutable, and therefore potentially infelicitous. At times the meaning is ironic: Hester intends it to mean something different to Pearl. The letter also ironically suggests both punishment and redemption, as when Hester pleads with Governor Bellingham that the scarlet letter pedagogically reforms her. Austin questions whether we can say things we do not really "mean" and yet be legally bound and responsible. Exposing the letter *A* to speech act theory raises the question of whether Hester always intends the letter to say what others think it means, and whether she believes in the force of her utterance when she first emerges into public. After all, the letter "had the effect of a spell, taking her out of the ordinary relations with humanity, and inclosing her in a sphere by herself."

To fellow Bostonians, Hester's wearing of the *A* appears to indicate that she complies with the juridical meaning of her punishment. But the possibility exists that she reassigns meaning to the *A* because the letter, to cite Butler's ideas about an utterance, "is uncontrollable, appropriable, and able to signify otherwise and in excess of its animating intentions" (98). By wearing her embroidered badge, Hester at once daily confesses her sin yet also perhaps holds back. It is not entirely clear that she believes she and Arthur sinned: in their meeting in the woods, Hester pleads to Arthur to escape with her because what they did "had a consecration of its own" (126). Considered in this light, the letter does *not* say what the magistrates want it to say. Thus, Hester and the magistrates must negotiate an "asymmetry of their abilities to perform certain illocutionary acts" (Langton 316).

Wearing the letter *A* enforces solitude, yet the isolation effected by the letter also grants Hester a certain intellectual freedom not accorded to the typical Puritan woman. Her unconstrained mind is free to wander: "Thoughts visited her, such as dared to enter no other dwelling in New England" (108). In some ways, her badge of shame represents a fortunate fall, for Hester has gained much knowledge through her suffering: "The scarlet letter was her passport into regions where other women dared not tread. Shame, Despair, Solitude! These had been her teachers" (128). But the letter's ability to denigrate and subordinate the hearer raises the question of whether Hester can simultaneously be both hearer of the magistrate's enforced *A* and the speaker of the *A* herself. Butler claims that in hate speech, "the listener is injured as a consequence of [the] utterance" (18). If, as a "living sermon" or the "text of the discourse," Hester herself and not the magistrates utters the *A*, does she consequently impart damage upon hearers of the letter? Butler further argues that injurious language "may also produce an unexpected and enabling response. If to be addressed is to be interpellated, then the offensive call runs the risk of inaugurating a subject in speech who comes to use language to counter the offensive call" (2). Thus, signifying on the *A* with her gold thread inaugurates Hester as a subject with a dissenting language.

Bercovitch points out that Hawthorne's initial suggestion about Hester's surrendering her individuality to become a symbol proves false: Hawthorne, Bercovitch claims, lets Hester asserts her individuality "through her capacity to make the general symbol her own," which constitutes "an act of appropriation through dissent" (152). By richly embroidering the *A* in gold thread that violates the Puritans' castigatory intention, Hester registers a forceful dissent. This signifying on the *A* raises questions about performative speech act theory regarding the concept of citation. In other words, is Hester sincerely uttering the *A* as her personal confession, or do her needlework skills indicate that she is merely quoting or citing the magistrates' intended punishment and thus initiating a different determining context and meaning?

According to Butler, "An aesthetic enactment of an injurious word may both *use* the word and *mention* it, that is, make use of it to produce certain effects but also at the same time make reference to that very use, calling attention to it as a citation, situating that use within a citational legacy, making that use into an explicit discursive item to be reflected on rather than a taken for granted operation of ordinary language" (99). Applying these ideas to Hester, we can see the heroine as "mentioning" the *A* and "making use" of it, rather than confessionally uttering it. Her gold-threaded dissent calls attention to the *A* and cites it, rather than using it as "an explicit discursive item." Laws work because they cite convention; they refer to practices permitted and prohibited by communal agreement. If Hester is citing the *A,* she is not performing the injurious language, but referring to and signifying upon the magistrates' speech from a step removed.

Miller argues that citing an utterance, rather than performing it, suspends its meaning (3). He argues that citation "is supposed to drag its original context implicitly along with it" (71). This property of citation is problematic in legislating against pornographic speech. In order to testify in court against the damaging effects of pornography, women must repeat the very injury they seek to suppress. Langton points out the regrettable irony that female victims who testify in court about being raped and sexually harassed learn that their descriptions of their experiences enact pornographic speech. They become guilty of speaking pornographically when they talk about their violation and find themselves without a forceful way to use language to counter the inherent violence of pornography. As Langton argues, "If pornography legitimates violence as sex, then it can silence the intended actions of those who want to testify about violence" (326).

If we view the letter *A* as a citation, we can see that Hester avoids reenacting the linguistic injury. Through citation, Hester drags along the letter's original meaning, but she dissents without legitimating the magistrates' verdict. Because the scarlet *A* accords with an accepted convention and has an accepted effect, it can be said to have "a sedimentation, a repetition that congeals, that gives the name its force" (Butler 36). Yet when Hester utters the gold-framed *A*, she does not re-sediment or re-congeal the meaning. Through the embroidered alphabetic, she refers to the letter's encoded memory but cites the *A* against itself and still insists that her affair with Dimmesdale had a "consecration of its own."

Many in the gay community have effected a similar turn by reclaiming the hate word *queer*. As Butler writes, "The revaluation of terms such as 'queer' suggests that speech can be 'returned' to its speaker in a different form, that it can be cited against its originary purposes, and perform a reversal of effects" (14). Hawthorne's readers can see Hester cite the *A*, signify on it, and reassign its authority to claim a position of strength. For example, Hawthorne writes, "The scarlet letter was her passport into regions where other women dared not tread" (128). As Hester utters her scarlet and gold dissent over time, townspeople begin "to look upon the scarlet letter as the token, not of that one sin, for which she had borne so long a dreary a penance, but of her many good deeds since" (106). Michael T. Gilmore's claim that "the townspeople forget the 'original signification' of Hester's letter because that original meaning—of woman as fallen Eve—has been eclipsed historically by middle-class woman's role as self-sacrificing dispenser of nurturance" (602) could be attributed to her persistent citation of the *A*. Hester's enduring citation causes the townsfolk to begin to soften towards her: "Society was inclined to show its former victim a more benign countenance than she cared to be favored with, or, perchance, than she deserved" (106). They view the letter as an emblem not of sin, but of good deeds, such that "the scarlet letter had the effect of the cross on a nun's bosom. It imparted to the wearer a kind of sacredness, which enabled her to walk securely amid all peril. Had she fallen among thieves, it would have kept her safe" (106). Some even report seeing the letter protect Hester from being pierced by an Indian's arrow (106).

Hester's citation of the *A* leads to the question of whether two other characters, Pearl and Dimmesdale, also cite the scarlet letter. Pearl's green seaweed *A* departs from legalized procedure and ritual and performs a highly unique speech act understood only by Hester, Pearl's intended audience. If, according to Austin, "the procedure must be executed by all participants correctly" (36), we can see Pearl's attempt as an infelicitous utterance because Hester does not believe it to be executed properly. Hester tells Pearl, "My little Pearl, the green letter, and on thy childish bosom, has no purport" (115). As a mark or utterance, the seaweed *A* carries no force. As a motherly response to Pearl, Hester explains her wearing of the scarlet letter: "And as for the scarlet letter, I wear it for the sake of its gold thread!" (117). This is not so flippant an answer as one might think, because its gold thread is part of its performative powers. While Hester thus avoids explaining to her daughter the sin of adultery, she accurately reveals that the gold-threaded *A* utters a dissent that makes it important to continue wearing.

Does Pearl thus cite the letter *A*? Perhaps a more accurate term might be that Pearl iterates the scarlet *A*. Iterability is "the possibility for every mark to be repeated and still to function as a meaningful mark in new contexts that are cut off entirely from the original context" (Miller 78). Pearl thus iterates the *A* because she does not mean to drag along the intended castigatory meaning. Her seaweed *A* repeats the iconography of the letter but constitutes it with a new, childish meaning that indicates a loving attempt to identify with her mother. As a mark, the *A* can be iterated in seaweed by a child. Pearl then links Hester's alphabetic sign to the manner in which Dimmesdale holds his hand over his heart.

This brings us to a key question that hands interpretation over to the reader: does Dimmesdale felicitously utter a confession in the novel's closing pages? Of course, Hawthorne plays with the reader by writing, "Most of the spectators testified to having seen, on the breast of the unhappy minister, a SCARLET LETTER—the very semblance of that worn by Hester Prynne—imprinted in the very flesh. As regarded its origin, there were various explanations, all of which must necessarily have been conjectural" (162). But this assertion that most viewers saw a red wound is countered in the next paragraph: "It is singular, nevertheless, that certain persons, who were spectators of the whole scene, and professed never once to have removed their eyes from the Reverend Mr. Dimmesdale, denied that there was any mark whatever on his breast, more than on a new-born infant's. Neither, by their report, had his dying words acknowledged, nor even remotely implied, any, the slightest connection, on his part, with the guilt for which Hester Prynne had so long worn the scarlet letter" (163).

Hawthorne teases readers about Dimmesdale's success in confessing. According to Austin, for a speech act to be felicitous, it must contain the right words said in the right circumstances to the right listeners. If we have been establishing that Hester's scarlet letter performatively speaks a confession, why doesn't Dimmesdale's self-flagellated scarlet letter also felicitously perform a confession? Butler claims, "A speech act can be an act without necessarily being an efficacious act. If I utter a failed performative, that is, I make a command and no one hears or obeys, I make a vow, and there is no one to whom or before whom the vow might be made, I still perform an act, but I perform an act with no or little effect" (16–17). If many spectators failed to see a fleshly *A* on Dimmesdale's breast, then perhaps the letter, if it existed, performed an act, but an ineffectual one.

Dimmesdale argues against Chillingworth's suggestion that unconfessed sin will spring forth from the sinner's grave as black weeds, claiming, "There can be . . . no power, short of the Divine mercy, to disclose, whether by uttered words, or by type or emblem, the secrets that may be buried with a human heart. . . . Nor have I so read or interpreted Holy Writ, as to understand that the disclosure of human thoughts and deed, then to be made [at the Judgment], is intended as a part of the retribution" (88). In other words, Dimmesdale maintains that since the confession of sin is not required by scripture, he doesn't need to admit any guilt. Chillingworth then tries to force a confession out of the minister, telling Hester, "He bears no letter of infamy wrought into his garment, as thou dost; but I shall read it on his heart" (54). Chillingworth's desire to extract such confession cannot produce a true admission of sin, for the words must come earnestly from the sinner's interior to his exterior.

Nonetheless, Dimmesdale tries to confess several times in the novel. Interestingly, the word "utter" appears four times in the chapter titled "The Leech and His Patient," as if Hawthorne were tinkering with the verbal link between sin and its absolution. Dimmesdale advises his physician that "uttered words" or emblems that reveal sin cannot be disclosed except by divine power (88). Eventually, Dimmesdale sermonizes, the heart will reveal secrets with a "joy unutterable." Chillingworth coyly asks the minister why the guilty should not take advantage of the "unutterable solace" to confess in private. Dimmesdale replies that men "shrink from displaying themselves black" and instead wander amidst "unutterable torment" (88).

Despite the emphasis on utterances, Dimmesdale fails to confess from his pulpit. The narrator reports, "More than once—nay, more than a hundred times—he had actually spoken! Spoken! But how? He had told his hearers that he was altogether vile, a viler companion than the vilest, the worst of sinners, an abomination. . . . Could there be plainer speech than this?. . . . They heard it all, and did but reverence him the more" (99). Dimmesdale's words do not enact a confession because he speaks in too general terms. While Hester's *A* persistently confesses her maternity, Dimmesdale fails to claim his paternity. In asking "Spoken! But how?" the narrator questions Dimmesdale's ability to mean what he says. His credibility as a truth-teller crumbles; when Dimmesdale tries to confess how vile he is, he appears all the more revered to his parishioners: "He had spoken the very truth, and transformed it into the veriest falsehood" (95–96).

Dimmesdale attempts a confession in chapter 12 on the pillory late at night, but only manages to utter a shriek in the empty town square (98). He thinks this suffices for a confession of the agony of his soul, for he exclaims, "It is done! . . . The whole town will awake, and hurry forth, and find me here!" (ibid.). Of course, no one serves as an audience for this scream. The next day he refuses Pearl's invitation to stand with her and her mother on the pillory, thus again failing to connect his shame to Hester's.

Without the right words being said at the right time to the right auditors under the right conditions, Dimmesdale cannot be said to have performed a felicitous illocutionary act. He may have tried to follow conventional procedures, but an unheard solitary shriek does not count as a proper execution; it does not "speak its purport." Ironically, Dimmesdale perhaps dies thinking he has confessed. However, as Dillingham points out, the townspeople have not realized the minister was an adulterer, because if the Puritan community knew of Hester and Dimmesdale's actual relationship, the two would not have been buried together under a shared tombstone (25).

The Scarlet Letter, with its appreciation of the differences between constative and performative aspects of the *A,* shows Hawthorne to be an early philosopher of speech act theory. The force of Hester's scarlet utterance can be examined along with its attendant impact on Hester's fellow townspeople and on theories of reading itself. Exposing the letter *A* to speech act theory helps readers understand how, as an utterance, the scarlet *A* affects and controls much of the action and perception in the novel, and how the letter *A,* as language, can have (again in Austin's terms) both felicitous and infelicitous effects on other characters and on the reader.

Although tenets of speech act theory became codified in the twentieth century, Ludwig Fleck argues that in intellectual history, ideas fully articulated in one period often appeared as "proto-ideas" in a previous period. Christopher Herbert summarizes Fleck: "Scientific theories have a kind of larval phase in which they exist as 'proto-ideas' or 'pre-ideas' often of a thoroughly superstitious character, embodied not in logical discourse but in emotionally loaded metaphors" (24). Following Fleck, an argument could be made that although Hawthorne wrote his novel unaware of performative speech theory, his ideas in *The Scarlet Letter* demonstrate a "larval phase" of such discourse and that Hawthorne understood the potency of linguistic utterances that would not be codified until a century after his death. Concurring with Michael Ragussis's claim that "Hawthorne and his characters imagine speech as an act of potency" (863), I would add that through his mystical symbol, Hawthorne examines how a pictogram of language, a specimen of speech, oscillates between communal and private, between being publicly held and personally owned, in order to demonstrate how to do things with a letter.

4

Verbal Violence in *Uncle Tom's Cabin*

This chapter proposes a new reading of an important but neglected scene in Harriet Beecher Stowe's *Uncle Tom's Cabin:* the scene in volume 2, chapter 33, in which Cassy defiantly challenges Sambo as he threatens to whip her for assisting Tom. I read this scene through the lens of performative speech theory to raise questions about the mutually constitutive nature of language and action that inheres in Stowe's strategy of sympathetic identification through domestic sentimentality. When viewed in light of performative speech theory, Cassy's insubordinate retort to Sambo both signals Stowe's understanding of the capacity of the upraised whip to elicit readers' sympathy and simultaneously challenges the firmament on which such sympathy can lie. Cassy's words, and Sambo's understanding of them, rupture Stowe's carefully constructed argument that champions ameliorative, reformatory language over force. I suggest that understanding Cassy's speech as performative revises and extends our understanding of Stowe's use of feminine sociomoral conversational pedagogy, and that it raises questions about where for Stowe (and other antebellum women writers) linguistic authority lies: in the suasive potential of sentiment, in the assaultive nature of words, or in the ways sentiment and assault mutually authorize each other.

The scene of concern to this chapter occurs as Cassy is picking cotton on Simon Legree's plantation. She observes newcomer Tom empathetically place some cotton he has picked into the basket of an ailing slave. Realizing Tom does not know that he endangers himself by helping a fellow slave, Cassy transfers to Tom's basket some of her own cotton, explaining, "You know nothing about this place . . . or you wouldn't have done that. When you've been here a month, you'll be done helping anybody" (322). Sambo, the acting slave driver, approaches Cassy, who resumes the backbreaking work. He brandishes his whip at her and sneers, "Go along! yer under me now,—mind yourself, or yer'll cotch it!" (ibid.). This is an iconic

81

moment: the crouching, hunched over, cotton-picking subservient slave threatened by a ready whip. Highly suggestive, this passage references repeated images that readers would regard as "untrammeled visualizations"—that is, truthful, mimetic images that convey reality unmediated by fictive technique (Morgan 1).[1]

An astute reader of literature and culture, Stowe borrowed and reworked numerous popular images and types. For example, *Uncle Tom's Cabin* incorporates popularly repeated figures such as the innocent dying child, the tragic mulatta, the fugitive mother with youngster, the minstrel performer, the evil slave owner, and the righteous matriarch. Yet another stock image Stowe employs is that of the slave about to be whipped. Marion Wilson Starling notes, "The figure of the fugitive slave, panting in a swamp with the slave holder brandishing a whip and surrounded by bloodhounds . . . became so popular as a symbol that dinner plates were made with the scene for a center motif; the handles of silverware were embossed with the story . . . and the fad even extended to the embellishment of transparent window blinds" (29). If this image had been codified for consumption by 1835, as Starling notes, then by mid-century Stowe's depiction of this scene would appear familiar and formulaic. Antebellum readers would no doubt recognize at once the power dynamics that inhere in the image of a slave woman being threatened by an overseer lifting his rawhide, especially since readers would likely have seen similar imagery on china plates, silverware, and window treatments.[2] The scene under discussion here elicits sympathy for poor Cassy's suffering and calls upon whites to feel outrage and indignation at her imminent abuse. Stowe wanted readers to feel for Cassy through sympathetic identification and thus be moved towards the abolitionist cause.[3]

Yet Cassy's response to Sambo challenges the way readers receive Stowe's sympathetic strategies. Cassy rages at the driver, "Touch *me*, if you dare! I've power enough, yet, to have you torn by the dogs, burnt alive, cut to inches! I've only to say the word!" This threat to "say the word" makes Sambo lower the punishing rod and retreat with a sullen, "Didn't mean no harm, Misse Cassy!" (322). What exactly is it that Cassy threatens to say? What words could make the holder of a whip cower? Cassy's threat to "say the word" is a threat to use language performatively to cast a vodun hex on Sambo.[4]

On a pragmatic level, readers could assume that Cassy believes she still has enough influence or power over Legree to convince him to whip Sambo. Presumably Cassy could report to Legree that Sambo has beaten her or made sexual advances; a jealous Legree might logically beat his upstart slave driver.[5] Yet this most obvious explanation of Cassy's words cannot fully encompass the scene's meanings because Cassy indicates that she could cause Sambo to suffer from more than a whipping: her words would cause dogs to tear him up and for fire to burn him alive. It is unlikely that, if Cassy were to report attempted sexual aggression, Legree would actually burn Sambo at the stake or chop him into little pieces. Further, were Cassy threatening Sambo with a false report of sexual aggression, Sambo could whip her doubly at some point in the future for leveling a devious charge. Something else in Cassy's words disarms Sambo so suddenly. What exactly is it that Sambo so definitely fears? Is Stowe saying that words could be more blistering than rawhide?

An examination of this scene through the lens of performative speech theory reveals that violent language may prove more efficacious than sentimental petitions. Cassy's threat to Sambo thus presents a compelling narrative question because, until this point in the novel and in numerous scenes afterward, Stowe presents moral suasion as the only viable alternative to violence. In the book's preface, Stowe tells her readers that her purpose is to "awaken sympathy and feeling for the African race" (xiii). Gregg Crane argues that "Stowe considered sentiment the medium of human conscience. One *feels* the conflict between the law of slavery and the higher law principles of the natural rights tradition" (178). Stowe's sentimental sympathetic strategy, however, falters with Cassy's utterance.

Critics have written extensively on Stowe's ability to use bourgeois sentimentality to craft an emotionally engaging and politically motivating story. Elizabeth Barnes cogently summarizes Stowe's strategy in her claim that "sympathy is made contingent upon similarity" (92). Marianne Noble argues that "the sentimental wound" is "a bodily experience of anguish caused by identification with the pain of another" (295). Glenn Hendler claims that sentiment is "premised on the possibility of a perfect intersubjectivity of affect" (145); thus, Stowe operated on the assumption that readers would feel moved by the sentiment inherent in a beautiful slave being unjustly whipped for assisting the novel's hero. Carolyn Sorisio cautions that many reform writers relied on "the sentimental assumption that corporeal pain is a universally understandable and translatable experience" (49).[6] Following sentimental tradition, Stowe crafts Cassy in such a way that readers can link themselves to her—perhaps by locating similarity in her oppression as a woman, her lovely features, her sympathetic outreach to Tom, a shared fear of corporeal wounding, or her plight as a slave (so familiar to antebellum readers).

Stowe solidifies her case for the "sympathetic influence" of sentimentality even when her own character's words fail. For example, in volume 1, chapter 9, Senator Bird hurries Eliza and Harry into a carriage to escape from pursuing slave hunters. In their final moment together, Mrs. Bird and Eliza are too overcome with emotion to exchange parting words: "Eliza leaned out of the carriage, and put out her hand,—a hand as soft and beautiful as was given in return. She fixed her large, dark eyes, full of earnest meaning, on Mrs. Bird's face, and seemed going to speak. Her lips moved,—she tried once or twice, but there was no sound" (80). Where words fall short, the clasp of hands speaks volumes. Aware that a corporeal appeal often works best, Stowe brilliantly demonstrates that when language fails, the physicality of unmediated emotions rings true.

Although *Uncle Tom's Cabin* was serialized in the abolitionist newspaper the *National Era* (from 5 June 1851–1 April 1852, before being published in volume form in March 1852), the *Era* had not published antislavery fiction until that date. Abolitionist ideas appeared almost exclusively in the form of poetry or essays. According to Barbara Hochman, fiction in the *Era* was didactic: "It tells the reader to be diligent and patient, to obey one's parents and trust Providence. It stresses the efficacy of individual will and the importance of emotional moderation, whether in love or death" (147). Until Stowe's work, fiction in the *Era* actually avoided depicting slavery. Since *Uncle Tom's Cabin* marked the first significant appearance in the *Era* of fiction as a vehicle for portraying slavery, the novel represented a departure from generic norms. It is important to recall that, as sentimental fiction, *Uncle Tom's Cabin* was revolutionary, for, as Hochman observes, it "established sympathetic identification as a widespread reading practice for consuming the story of slavery" (144). That such sympathetic identification established a far-reaching fictive strategy for abolitionism is important when considering the way Cassy's retort to Sambo reinforces yet destabilizes Stowe's narrative aims.

Cassy's threat to "say the word" demonstrates the power of performative speech—that is, speech that does not merely describe a situation but, as Jacques Derrida says, "produces or transforms a situation" (*Limited Inc* 13). In other words, Sambo finds Cassy's speech so menacing because Cassy does not merely threaten to describe or report a future action; she warns that she has the power to articulate words that will lead to, or will themselves be, an action with violent results. Her threat shows readers "how to do things with words" to save herself from a beating.

In this scene, language reveals itself to be a force: words need not honorably convince but can constitute action powerful enough to meet violence with violence. Assaultive language proves more expeditious than persuasive language. As discussed in the introduction, speech act theory relies on Austin's distinctions between "perlocutionary" speech and "illocutionary" speech, with perlocutionary speech being constantive speech that reports or describes the world, while illocutionary speech is that which performs an action (109–10). An examination of Cassy's ability to cause violence through an utterance reveals links between her illocutionary speech and New World vodun.

Cassy's ability to cast a hex, or evil spell, derives from the rich syncretic New Orleans milieu in which she lives. Since Cassy is a woman who uses speech *not* for its capacity for moral tutelage but for its performative force, giving Cassy such verbal power demands that readers sympathetically identify with a conjure woman who uses speech differently from other women in the novel. I will examine Stowe's nods toward black diasporic culture to contextualize Cassy's performative speech and to suggest how Cassy's performative utterance weakens Stowe's investment in sympathetic identification.

In the late eighteenth century, slaves and free blacks from Haiti and Cuba retained West African religious practices including vodun, which became enmeshed with aspects of Catholicism, including saints' holidays and veneration of icons. Vodun in New Orleans reached its height around 1850 and particularly endowed blacks and women with spiritual powers (see Fessenden and Raboteau). Anna Brickhouse describes Cassy as "New Orleans–born, French-speaking, possessed of magical powers associated with vodun, and unwilling mistress to a man who 'learned his trade well, among the pirates in the West Indies'" (430). Including vodun in such an overtly Christian text could run Stowe into trouble, for although Raboteau claims that "conjure was not always employed for evil" (287), he does argue that the "practice of conjure was, at least in theory, in conflict with

Christian beliefs about the providence of God, and indeed one way of relating conjure to Christianity was to make the former the realm of the devil" (286).

Uncle Tom's Cabin is characterized by what Brickhouse calls the "Franco-Africanist shadow cast by New Orleans and its proximity to Haiti and the larger West Indies" (430). She rightly points out the several places the Franco-Caribbean world impinges on the novel's concerns. For example, as Brickhouse points out, George Harris questions the ability of Haiti to serve as a stable, independent nation. He demands "a people that shall have a tangible, separate existence of its own; and where am I to look for it?" (374). He answers his own question, "Not in Hayti, for in Hayti they had nothing to start with. . . . The race that formed the character of the Haytiens was a worn-out, effeminate one; and, of course, the subject race will be centuries in rising to anything" (ibid.). Haiti also figures in Augustine St. Clare's thoughts when, about the possibility of slave revolts, he muses, "If ever the San Domingo hour comes, Anglo-Saxon blood will lead the day" (234). Brickhouse reminds us that although Eliza and George's son Harry was born in English-speaking Kentucky, "the novel's conclusion places him securely in the francophone world of Louisiana, revealing him as none other than the grandson of the tragic quadroon Cassy," and that little Harry ends up being the nephew of Cassy's mixed-race son Henry, who was sold in New Orleans but reappears by novel's end (430). Finally, as Brickhouse notes, Stowe also includes George Harris's sister, Madame de Thoux, the former slave and wife of a West Indian Creole owner, who is passing as a French woman (431).

With this Franco-Africanist shadow hovering over Cassy, readers view Cassy and her utterance in the context of a New Orleans diasporic belief system. Derrida suggests that a performative utterance draws agency by following a code or by being identified as a "citation" (*Limited Inc* 12). In other words, Cassy's threat can be seen as legitimate or "coded" in that it derives its force from its context within an established, recognizable tradition of vodun. Furthermore, "the particular persons and circumstances in a given case must be appropriate for the invocation of the particular procedure involved" (Austin 15).

Legree's slave driver immediately understands the implications of Cassy's speech act and, therefore, why her speech has the potential to be assaultive. Cassy's ability to curse Sambo exists within the "accepted conventional procedure" of vodun practice. Were Sambo unfamiliar with hexes, Cassy's utterance would be "infelicitous." Her language would fail to be performative if Sambo were not "appropriate for the invocation." A failure to understand Cassy's assaultive language would constitute what Austin calls a misinvocation, a misapplication, or a misexecution (17). Thus, when Cassy threatens to "say the word," Sambo immediately understands the volatility of language and believes in Cassy's powers to bring violence about, just as Cassy places credibility in Sambo's threat to lash the whip. Cassy and Sambo meet in an understanding of the corporeal harm latent in disciplinary tools, whether linguistic or leather.

Derrida builds on Austin's groundwork by recognizing the repetitive or copycat nature of performative speech. He asks, "Could a performative succeed if its formulation did not repeat a 'coded' or iterable utterance, or in other words, if the formula that I pronounce in order to open a meeting, launch a ship or a marriage were not identifiable as *conforming* with an iterable model, if it were not then identifiable in some way as a 'citation'?" (*Limited Inc* 18). Therefore, Austin's "uttering of certain words" that are "appropriate for the invocation" and that have "a certain conventional effect" stands as appropriate and conventional because the words have been heard before: they are repeated from one situation to the next and thereby aggregate in authority and currency. A hex in a foreign language or a curse of nonsense syllables may misfire because the hearer cannot understand. "Language," according to Jonathan Culler, "is performative in the sense that it doesn't just transmit information but performs acts by its repetition of established discursive practices or ways of doing things" (98). Cassy's performative language, then, relies on its iterability: in order for it to be felicitous, it must be a repetition of a previously successful curse drawn from a rich vodun heritage. Following Derrida, such language would be a citation, or a quoted extract, of supernatural conjure that follows a certain code within established vodun practice.

These points about felicity of utterance and citation are worth stressing because, just as Cassy's assaultive language relies on Sambo's understanding of its corrosive force, Stowe likewise relies on her readers' understanding of Sambo's reaction and on readers' ability to situate the novel in a New Orleans context of fluid and diasporic religious traditions. If readers failed to understand that Cassy could level a debilitating verbal curse, then Sambo's acceding to Cassy's threat would not make sense. To make Cassy's utterance felicitous, Stowe casts her readers as part of a community cognizant, and to a degree accepting, of the powers of vodun.

We can see Stowe acknowledging her readers' acquaintance with vodun in *A Key to Uncle Tom's Cabin*. Here, Stowe reflects popular knowledge of vodun "codes" when she writes, "The African race, in their own climate, are believers in spells, in 'fetish' and 'obi,' in 'the evil eye,' and other singular influences" (28). Speaking about "the African race," Stowe further reveals readers' familiarity with African folk belief when she writes, "We are not surprised to find almost constantly, in the narrations of their religious histories, accounts of visions, of heavenly voices, of mysterious sympathies and transmissions of knowledge from heart to heart without the intervention of the senses" (ibid.).

The use of fetishes in *Uncle Tom's Cabin,* and characters' appropriate reactions of fear or respect, suggests mid-century readers' acquaintance with African folk belief. For example, in volume 2, chapter 35, Simon Legree reacts hysterically when Sambo presents him with "a witch thing"— "something that niggers get from witches. Keeps 'em from feelin' when they's flogged. [Tom] had it tied round his neck, with a black string" (338). Sambo opens the package to reveal Tom's souvenirs of a silver dollar and a lock of Eva's hair. Recognizing the hair's totemic power, Legree screams for Sambo to "burn it up!—burn it up! . . . Don't you bring me any more of your devilish things" (ibid.).[7] Dinah keeps possible occult tokens such as a bloody cloth and sweet herbs in her kitchen drawers, which remind readers of her still-vital connection to African cultural praxis (Wardley 204). Further, Stowe describes Cassy in demonic terms: she has a strange "influence" over Legree (321), who calls her a "she-devil" (337), and Cassy herself claims, "I've got the devil in me!" (ibid.).

Such inclusions of fetish, obi, tokens, witchery, conjure, influence, and devilry provide a vodun context in which Cassy's utterance can succeed felicitously. These West African beliefs in harnessing supernatural powers were introduced into white America by slaves and immeasurably affected white society and faith. For example, as a white, middle-class woman, Stowe typified her social strata's interest in mediumship, mesmerism, and spiritualism by her participation in séances and her experimentation with a planchette, which Wardley describes as an "ouija-board-like instrument designed for extraworldly communication" (208). Wardley argues that the "retention of African cultural practices" among slaves has left "more traces on the aesthetics of sentiment in the United States than we have yet imagined" (204). She goes on to write, "Stowe's belief that some spirit inhabits all things is not only an exoticized import from the Roman Catholic and

African American religions of New Orleans and beyond. It is by 1852 one familiar element of the nineteenth-century domestic ideology the tenets of which Stowe's writing reflected and helped to shape" (205). Wardley makes the insightful argument, important for my interests here, that Stowe's "recurrent representation of the uncanny power of Victorian material culture to elicit emotion, provoke somatic response, bewitch, heal, or avenge wrong, resonates not only with the Catholic faith in the power of relics, but also with the Pan-African religions of the antebellum South" (ibid.).

For an article on the planchette, Stowe gathered materials that she described to her editor James T. Fields as "really very extraordinary" (quoted in Hedrick 339). Stowe also tried contacting her dead son, Henry; claimed she held counsel with the spirit of Charlotte Brontë (Wardley 208); and believed a spiritualist medium received a "supposed communication" from her wayward son Fred (quoted in Hedrick 391). Russ Castronovo identifies Stowe's interest in mesmerism in the way that George Harris seems to cast a hypnotic spell over Mr. Wilson: George's former employer becomes "like one speaking in a dream" (97) and Stowe writes that Wilson follows George "as one who walks in his sleep" (98; quoted in Castronovo 15).

In light of Wardley's discussion, bourgeois sentimentalism seems to bewitch or cast a charm or spell. Far from standing as a chaste, unpolluted stronghold against alien West African magic and slave culture, white domesticity to some extent shares vodun's tenet of animism. Lori Merish argues that as a hallmark of sentimental materialism, "domestic material culture is represented in great detail and . . . personal possessions are endowed with psychological or characterological import" (139). In her explanation of the power of fetish in *Uncle Tom's Cabin,* Gillian Brown writes of the "transformative capacity of sentimental possession" (48) and suggests that "Stowe's sentimental fetishism invests domestic possessions with [a] sense of empathy between the object and its owner" (51), so that there exists "a reciprocity between persons and their possessions, by seeing them as contiguous and congruent" (52). For example, sentimentalism grants totemic value to objects to evoke a lost loved one: recall the tears elicited by Mrs. Bird when she gives her dead son's toys to fugitive Harry, or the potent after-death conjuring power of Eva's and Legree's mother's locks of hair. Brown argues that "the memorial lock of hair Simon Legree's mother left him operates to abet the escape of Cassy and Emmeline and to render him powerless. So powerful is this sentimental possession that its influence survives and strengthens in its disposal" (50).

This homology between sentimental bourgeois possessivism and the entrancing nature of fetishized objects facilitates readers' bonds to Cassy and her bewitching powers. Raboteau links African and Christian religions in his claim that "Christian tradition itself has always been attuned to special gifts (charisms) of the Spirit as they are manifested in prophecy, healing, and miracles. . . . In an important sense, conjure and Christianity were not so much antithetical as complementary" (287). Cassy's close link to conjure and vodun thus threatens to rupture Stowe's vision of a salvific Christianity, for how can a vodun practitioner receive God's grace? To erase Cassy's New World African diasporic heritage by the end of the novel, Stowe has Cassy implore in chapter 40, "If God would give me back my children, then I could pray" (374). To show that a benevolent God rewards those with moral righteousness, when Stowe restores Cassy's children to her in chapter 43, Cassy "yield[s] at once, and with her whole soul, to every good influence, and be[comes] a devout and tender Christian" (392).

Cassy's threat to performatively "say the word" thus problematizes Stowe's aim of eschewing violence in favor of matrifocal sympathetic conversion because Cassy's speech act so clearly succeeds in its execution. At the same time, however, the efficacy of Cassy's performativity relies on bourgeois sentimentalism's derivation from the very conjure that enables Cassy's words. Thus, Cassy's threat to use speech performatively to cast a hex may resonate for readers who, because of vodun's syncretic influence, are familiar with the inspirited, corporeal relationships that inhere among words, objects, and feelings.

Much of Stowe's writing can be described as "domestic didactics" that deploy "feminine sociomoral influence" (Robbins 535). As Sarah Robbins writes, "Stowe learned how to use a tutelary voice in print to create layers of conversation-centered learning in her narratives—to help position readers as participants in a mother-to-learner talk *about* the text's own vivid verbal tableaux of domestic, conversational pedagogy in action" (543). By deploying this strategy of using dialogic exchange to attempt to shape morality, "Stowe was adapting for her antislavery narrative a recognizable approach she had already exploited in earlier domestic didactic stories" (ibid.). We can therefore view Cassy as modeling a different—performative—way to engage language and bring about social change. As readers, we eavesdrop on Cassy's instructive use of the efficacy of assaultive language. By saving her from an immediate beating, such belligerent language supplants a maternal, gently suasive, tutelary voice. Cassy's utterance to Sambo retains Stowe's tried and true method of dialogic learning as Cassy teaches readers that performative utterances (although not necessarily of vodun hexes) can stave off a beating and garner respect from men and sympathy from women readers.

Yet Cassy's utterance also greatly revises Stowe's previous modeling of sympathetic identification because the performative nature of Cassy's language relies on its assaultive, not suasive, force. Cassy's threat to "say the word" removes readers from the paradigm of moral conversion because, as Eve Allegra Raimon has written, "Cassy's capacity for violence and incendiary speech places her outside conventional literary parameters" (111). Cassy does not use language to ask Sambo to "see . . . to [his] sympathies" or to create an "atmosphere of sympathetic influence," as Stowe does in her concluding chapter (*Uncle Tom's* 385). Rather, Cassy meets Sambo's whip with something equally brutalizing: assaultive language with injurious, not suasive, powers. Since this scene is the first time we meet Cassy, her "resistant orality" (a term coined by Harryette Mullen and cited by Raimon [111]) creates a hitherto unmatched rich portrayal of black female subjectivity. Sambo recognizes the violence inherent in Cassy's speech and lowers his whip.

George Shelby also makes clear the violence inherent in certain verbal utterances at the end of the novel. For example, the word "nigger" proves so assaultive that it demands a similar response. When George threatens to have Legree charged with the murder of Tom, Legree sneers that no witnesses exist since blacks cannot testify against whites. Legree says scornfully, "After all, what a fuss, for a dead nigger." The narrative continues, "The word was as a spark to a powder magazine. Prudence was never a cardinal virtue of the Kentucky boy. George turned, and, with one indignant blow, knocked Legree flat upon his face" (383). Although the epithet is not hurled against George himself, he viscerally feels the punch of the hate speech and returns the attack. Jonathan Arac comments on this scene, claiming "a major point of *Uncle Tom's Cabin* has been to bring good-hearted white folks to realize that 'nigger' is a fighting word" (29).

Cassy's assaultive language presents a dilemma. On the one hand, Stowe's mid-nineteenth-century readers should no longer feel a sentimental attachment to Cassy as she demonstrates volatile powers alien to the middle-class white reader. White women in particular—taught to be the angel of the house, inculcated with the tenets of true womanhood, and raised to be the calm, moral center of domestic life—would have great difficulty accessing Cassy's caustic, insubordinate speech. Sympathetic identification with Cassy should, at this point, fail.

On the other hand, the aggression of a black woman's actions could be enjoyed as a fantasy for white women, including Stowe herself, who lacked social enfranchisement to hold such supremacy or command. Hochman argues, "Images of slave experience invited readers to identify with modes of behavior that were beyond the pale of white middle-class life, or at least prescriptions for it. The pleasure derived from such identifications would necessarily be multiple and complex; but *Uncle Tom's Cabin* encouraged white mothers to try circuiting themselves through black ones in order to imagine states of feeling systematically forbidden to them" (154).

Whites "circuiting" themselves through blacks constitutes a type of blackface enjoyment. By speaking through Cassy, Stowe pleasurably experiences the assaultive nature of speech. Indeed, Stowe gains authority for her gender in a way that she never directly claims through her white characters. Sarah Meer argues that "the minstrel elements of Stowe's book may have facilitated its rereading and rewriting by drawing on the inherent instabilities and ambivalences in the racial politics of blackface" (9). In *Uncle Tom's Cabin,* Cassy's performativity contributes to this aura of unstable racial politics by inviting readers at once to sympathize sentimentally with the iconic, submissive, rod-threatened slave and to thrill to the violence of resistant verbal action safely attributed to a black person.

Through Cassy, Stowe presents a different use of speech to bring about social change. This distinction matters because Stowe uses Cassy to model the success of assaultive language, not of suasive sentimentality. The nineteenth-century cult of domesticity that emphasized matrifocal sympathetic conversion as an abolitionist tool is undermined in this scene as readers see the benefit of using speech performatively as an action rather than as description. Cassy's words are more than a mere expression of anger. Because her utterance is itself an act of violence, she does not just express anger—her words have a force that can be understood as action. In this scene, Cassy's language does not merely convey emotion; it is an action with violent results.[8]

Cassy's performative utterance in this scene encapsulates in miniature Stowe's larger challenge as a woman attempting to assume a tone of power and consequence in a culture that ennobled a man's sermonic voice. As a woman, Stowe was not enfranchised to give moral instruction to men; according to Dawn Coleman, the writer George Frederick Holmes even took Stowe to task for violating scripture by not remaining silent and for usurping authority by attempting to teach men (265). From her minister father, Stowe acquired an appreciation of the way that sensational rhetoric bullied parishioners to conversion and the way that language, however flexible or fictional, could be used to bring out truths. Yet she struggled with a woman's lack of cultural permission similarly to arouse listeners with exhortations. As Robyn Warhol recognizes, through her maternal, sentimental language in *Uncle Tom's Cabin,* Stowe found a way to transform "a masculine means of enforcing spiritual presence into a feminine strategy for evoking presence in fiction" (108). Cassy's threat shows us that by granting verbal power to a doubly disenfranchised human—a woman and a slave—Stowe uses language both to evoke a feminine presence of sentiment with which readers identify and sympathize, and to assume the fiery, compelling challenge akin to that of a masculine pulpit minister.

Stowe's oscillation between sentimental maternal suasion and vitriolic performative speech, so succinctly encapsulated in Cassy, underscores Stowe's ambivalence about the role of the speaking woman. On the one hand, Stowe abided by the nineteenth-century convention of the demure woman: even when she toured Europe in the 1850s, she did not speak before mixed crowds (Coleman 289). Furthermore, Stowe knew that abolitionist rhetoric represented a challenge to the prevailing authorities. According to Michael T. Gilmore, "Measures, often violent, to censor abolitionist agitation as seditious and 'incendiary' (the preferred adjective) brought home the potentially lethal energy of words to all the antebellum authors, including those . . . who were themselves alarmed by the threat that anti-slavery oratory posed to the Union" (59). But by later claiming that God wrote the novel, Stowe cannily distanced herself from masculine (especially her father's) disapproval of her outspoken ideas.[9]

Clearly Stowe claims a consequential, influential voice in her novel: the immediacy of her characters' heartfelt situations and the beseeching prayers of the narrator elicit readers' tears. Much has been written about *Uncle Tom's Cabin* as an extended sermon.[10] As Coleman points out, adopting sermonic rhetoric proved to be a useful strategy for Stowe because "preaching was the voice of ultimate conviction in the antebellum United States—a nexus of oratorical style, biblical language, and personal presence that, sanctified by the rituals of the Protestant worship service, had tremendous potential to effect individual and social transformation" (266). Since preaching was forbidden for respectable middle-class white women, and particularly was opposed in Stowe's case by Lyman Beecher, Stowe could safely arouse the public to action in the guise of a pressing, imploring, motherly narrator. Rather than alarming a congregation from a pulpit, Stowe proffered her radical political vision of cross-racial sympathy and abolition to her readers within the normative constraints of domestic sentimentality.

Yet readers can also detect Stowe's ambivalence about empowered women's speech by reading Cassy's scene in light of what one could argue are the two different endings of *Uncle Tom's Cabin*—the published novel's ending and the serialized form's ending. The book version ends with a fire-and-brimstone vision of what James Baldwin called "theological terror, the terror of damnation" (498). Stowe pulls out all the big guns of a frightful sermon: she writes of a "day of vengeance," reveals how the "day shall burn as an oven" (adapting a quotation from Malachi 4.1), warns of the "wrath of an Almighty God," and calls for "repentance, justice and mercy" (408). The book ends on more of a doom-and-gloom note than many nineteenth-century preachers dared to intone in their sermons, which, according to Coleman, often ended with some sort of uplifting, hopeful message (277).

For a woman with strong political and religious convictions who was denied the chance to ascend her own pulpit, this mighty ending likely proved deeply gratifying and cathartic, similar to the satisfaction Stowe could take in vicariously speaking with force through Cassy. Both Stowe's concluding sermon and her slave-mother character offered Stowe the ventriloquist's pleasure of assuming a voice she dared not claim for herself. It was much safer to distance herself from an incendiary message by wearing the mask of a preacher or a sassy slave. But the book's sermonic ending differs from the ending readers encountered in the serialized version. Readers who followed Stowe's novel in the *National Era* found in the final installment on 1 April 1852 the following afterword:

> The "Author of Uncle Tom's Cabin" must now take leave of a wide circle of friends, whose faces she has never seen, but whose sympathies, coming to her from afar, have stimulated and cheered her in her work.
> The thought of the pleasant family circles that she has been meeting

in spirit weekly has been a constant refreshment to her, and she cannot leave them without a farewell.

In particular, the dear little children who have followed her story have her warmest love. Dear children, you will one day be men and women; and she hopes that you will learn from this story always to remember and pity the poor and oppressed, and, when you grow up, show your pity by doing all you can for them. Never, if you can help it, let a colored child be shut out of school, or treated with neglect and contempt, because of his color. Remember the sweet example of little Eva, and try to feel the same regard for all that she did; and then, when you grow up, we hope that the foolish and unchristian prejudice against people, merely on account of their complexion, will be done away with.

Farewell, dear children, till we meet again. (53)

The tone of this afterword seems to recant the wrathful, near-apocalyptic ending of the book by replacing it with a kind, sedate, moral, affectionate, (grand)motherly one. Gone are the hellish, punishing images; instead, readers find a "wide circle of friends," "dear little children," "pity," and a call to remember Eva's "sweet example" and thereby avoid prejudicial judgment. This final installment uses language to create a mutually supportive sphere of warmth, and to bind readers and writer conversationally together in a sentimental, domestic, instructive mission. How can these two widely divergent endings flow from the same pen?

I suggest that Stowe's wrestling with the tension between the tone and function of language in these two endings parallels her struggle with Cassy's use of language. In all cases, Stowe must decide how a woman speaks: Can she use forceful, compelling language to enact social change (as in the masculine sermonic rhetoric of the book version and Cassy's conjuring performative speech)? Or must she demur to the authorities (as in the patriarchal norms of feminine decorum in the serialized ending and the suasive sentiment modeled by Mrs. Shelby, Mrs. Bird, Rachel Halliday, Eva, Tom, Eliza, and others)? By penning two distinct endings to *Uncle Tom's Cabin,* Stowe flexed her ministerial muscle in the book version, but then recomposed her proper voice of a good housewife and mother a week later for the *National Era.* Similarly, through Cassy's performative utterance, Stowe departs from women's assigned appropriate voice and instead co-opts men's access to controlling speech. Cassy's performative speech diminishes her male challenger and forces him to back down and assent to her dominance. Yet this model of woman's speech by no means prevails in the novel, and by the story's end Cassy's reunion with her long-lost children converts her to an acquiescing mother and Christian. In Cassy and in the alternative endings, Stowe experiments with women's powerful speech but then safely frames it with normative domesticity.

Stowe's awareness of how to do things forcefully with words is transmuted in an interesting way in the hands of African American dramatist Robert Alexander in his 1991 play *I Ain't Yo' Uncle: The New Jack Revisionist Uncle Tom's Cabin,* in which the characters of Stowe's novel put Stowe on trial for creating damaging racist stereotypes. These "literary refugees," as Samual Otter calls them (16), continue the long tradition of African American rejoinders to *Uncle Tom's Cabin*.[11] I am most interested in Alexander's reimagining of Cassy's words when she is threatened with an attack. He recasts the scene slightly by having Simon Legree, not Sambo, hostilely confront Cassy. Tired of seeing Tom being brutalized by their master, Cassy pulls a gun on Legree, who sneers at her, "Nigger, you wouldn't dare" (88). Upon hearing the epithet *nigger,* Cassy replies, "I'm tired of hearing that word." The stage directions read, "She blows him away." When Alexander's character Harriet protests, "This is not the ending I wrote!," Cassy interjects, "You wrote every word of the rage that's in me. You just didn't give me a gun" (ibid.).

I am interested in Cassy's explosive, trigger-pulling response to Legree's insult. When read against Stowe's original version, I would argue that Alexander's Cassy, who responds by pulling the trigger, performatively speaks. Legree's use of the word *nigger* exemplifies illocutionary hate speech because, as Judith Butler argues, a fighting word such as *nigger "constitutes* its addressee at the moment of its utterance; it does not describe an injury or produce one as a consequence; it is, in the very speaking of such speech, the performance of the injury itself, where the injury is understood as social subordination" (18). Butler also asks, "What kind of power is *attributed to* speech such that speech is figured as having the power to constitute the subject with such success?" (19). Discussing Mari Matsuda's theories of hate speech, Butler writes, "A social structure is enunciated at the moment of the hateful utterance; hate speech reinvokes the position of dominance, and reconsolidates it at the moment of utterance" (ibid.). In this light, Legree's racial slur stands as a hateful act of asserting a social structure of dominance that likewise produces an injury. Legree relies on the racial epithet to be "coded" (in Derrida's sense, as mentioned above) in order to "constitute a subject [here, Cassy] through discursive means" (Butler 19).

Without its loaded, painful history from which to cite, the epithet *nigger* would fail to perform felicitously. Legree wounds Cassy with words; his words enact an injury through their performative force.

In Alexander's play, the character of Cassy does not threaten to perform an illocutionary speech act that will cause injury. She does not threaten to "say the word" as in Stowe's version. Instead, she "speaks" in a lethal way: she shoots a gun. Nor does the character Harriet recognize the ending of her own play. However, Cassy recognizes the potential of her violence that perhaps Harriet fails to see. In other words, Cassy believes her words in *Uncle Tom's Cabin* to be the result of rage as explosive as a gun; thus, her appropriate and equivalent response to Legree's use of the word *nigger* is to shoot. She uses shooting as a figure for speech; the performativity of the speaking gun injures Legree just as *nigger* performs an act of violence.

In *I Ain't Yo' Uncle* the playwright does not speak in blackface, as one could accuse Stowe of doing via Cassy or other black characters. Alexander recasts Topsy as a streetwise, fast-talking hip hop rapper. Not a minstrel performer, Alexander's Topsy directly addresses whites' fears. She sasses, "I oughta fuck you up! I see the way you look at me when I get on the bus . . . you sit there, scared" (89). While not threatening to assault whites, Alexander's Topsy reverses the blackface tradition: rather than white performers claiming to speak for blacks, this scene shows a black character giving voice to whites, in this case about whites' secret fears of black violence.

This returns us to Cassy's threat to the slave driver that she will "say the word." Although performative speech theory was not theorized or codified until the twentieth century, Stowe nonetheless demonstrates an awareness of the power of an utterance to be an action with assaultive force. As the daughter and sister of preachers known for their roiling, mordant sermonizing style, Stowe grew up aware of the power of "the word"—whether of God or of His earthly intermediaries—to strike fear in the hearts of believers. She understood that sympathetic identification moves readers to tears or stirs their emotions such that, as Stowe writes in the final chapter of *Uncle Tom's Cabin*, "*they feel right.* An atmosphere of sympathetic influence encircles every human being; and the man or woman who *feels* strongly, healthily and justly, on the great interests of humanity, is a constant benefactor to the human race" (404). In this last chapter, Stowe mightily summarizes what she has been advocating all along: domestic sentimentality and moral Christian feeling, rather than violence, should powerfully alter public judgment about slavery. Stowe, like other sentimental writers, believed that words could create an "atmosphere of sympathetic influence" sufficient enough to sway morality and peacefully instigate social change.

Stowe therefore simultaneously advocates the power of words to encourage readers to "feel right" against the institution of slavery yet also acknowledges that, because actions sometimes speak louder than words, performative speech may demonstrate more potent linguistic agency than sentimentalism and sympathetic identification. Cassy's brief scene exemplifies a larger linguistic dilemma: readers see that Stowe's committed reliance on women's suasive sentimentality quavers when she introduces the efficacy of assaultive language. By "circuiting" through a black woman's "unruly tongue,"[12] white middle-class readers momentarily experience the thrill of the violent potential in language. Similarly, by "circuiting" through a pulpit minister's voice in the book form of the novel, Stowe and her women readers vicariously enjoy preaching a message of moral and social reform in a powerful, hounding voice. Performatively, Cassy's threat to Sambo in *Uncle Tom's Cabin* equals a speaking gun or the force of George Shelby's indignant fist.

5

Action and Injurious Speech in *Moby-Dick*

With its emphasis on Ahab's vengeance, sailors' feats, and the white whale's exploits, *Moby-Dick* has invited many comments on scenes of action in the novel and the representation of masculine adventure. For many readers, the *Pequod*'s voyage exemplifies active derring-do and bravura. As one early reviewer remarked, Melville makes us "feel the sea breezes playing through our hair, the salt spray dashing on our brows" ("Fascination" 603). Yet many other readers have found the scenes of action to be subordinated to the lengthy discursive meditations on all things cetological—the shape of whales' heads, the manner in which they spout, the characteristics of their tails, and so on. For example, one early commentator wrote, "In all the scenes where the whale is the performer or the sufferer, the delineation and action are highly vivid and exciting. In all other respects, the book is sad stuff, dull and dreary, or ridiculous" (Simms 624).

This bifurcated view of the novel—both action-packed and yet slow and ponderous—represents much of the history of the criticism of *Moby-Dick*, and points to questions about the status of action itself in the novel. While Melville does indeed portray movement, action, and escapade, he shows himself to be even more interested in ruminating on action, or, as one could say, the act of acting. I am particularly interested in examining Melville's concern with the potential for language not just to represent action but to be action itself. By reading some scenes of *Moby-Dick* through some language theorists, particularly J. L. Austin and Judith Butler for their theories of the force of language, I hope to demonstrate how Melville troubles the distinction between words and action so that speech stands as an active agent and, in fact, acts to resist the wounding that results from injurious language itself.[1]

This interest in language as action begins with the scene in chapter 29 in which the second mate, Stubb, cannot sleep because Ahab is pacing the deck too loudly. Evidently Ahab is often mindful of the whalemen who are "seeking repose within six inches of his ivory heel," but this night "with heavy, lumber-like pace he was measuring the ship from taffrail to mainmast," thus keeping Stubb from a good night's sleep (111). The novel does not record Stubb's direct speech to Ahab; Melville instead couches Stubb's hesitancy in third-person narration: Stubb "hinted that if Captain Ahab was pleased to walk the planks, then, no one could say nay; but there might be some way of muffling the noise; hinting something indistinctly and hesitatingly about a globe of tow, and the insertion into it, of the ivory heel." The narrating voice then registers a regretful aside, lamenting that Stubb did not know Ahab's short temper: "Ah! Stubb, thou did'st not know Ahab then" (ibid.).[2]

Ahab roars his refusal to pace the deck more quietly by asking Stubb, "Am I a cannon-ball, Stubb . . . that thou wouldst wad me that fashion?" (ibid.). His subsequent orders to Stubb to return to his rest suggest death and oblivion: "Below to thy nightly grave; where such as ye sleep between shrouds" (ibid.). Ahab's instant refusal of his second mate's request approaches homosexual aggression (as if Stubb wanted to "wad" Ahab—I will return to this theme later). As if these denials were not enough, Ahab then sums his response to Stubb's presumed insolence by snarling, "Down, dog, and kennel!" (ibid.). Stubb, startled by Ahab's "unforeseen concluding lamentation," is speechless for a moment and then directly tells Ahab, "I am not used to be spoken to that way, sir" and that he "will not tamely be called a dog." Ahab retorts, "Then be called ten times a donkey, and a mule, and an ass, and begone, or I'll clear the world of thee!" (ibid.).

There is nothing unusual about such heated exchanges of words on board a ship between a superior and a subordinate. In fact, in chapter 54, when Radney orders Steelkilt to get a shovel and clean up pig feces, Ishmael tells us that the order "was almost as plainly meant to sting and insult Steelkilt, as though Radney had spat in his face" (204). However, the order is not uttered in a performative way; no physical injury results, but Steelkilt stews over the insulting incident, starts a mutiny, and glowers with self-justified pleasure when Moby-Dick devours Radney. Ahab also demonstrates an understanding of the way strong language can elicit anger in the auditor: in Ahab's famous "little lower layer" speech in chapter 36, he tries to diffuse the irritation he realizes he has stirred in Starbuck: "But look ye, Starbuck, what is said in heat, that thing unsays itself. There are men from whom warm words are small indignity. I meant not to incense thee. Let it go" (140). Ahab postulates that "warm words" growled by men cause only slight annoyances for some; further, words pronounced hastily in a heated exchange can be easily retracted or "unsaid." Acknowledging the transient nature of unthinking affronts, Ahab claims that words do not permanently wound. Apologizing for inadvertently incensing Starbuck, he asks his first mate to let the insult go. Stubb, however, cannot let go of Ahab's warm words; Ahab's insult to Stubb performatively wounds. Because Ahab thinks one can "unsay" words, he does not understand that his utterance performatively "kicks."

In the scene in chapter 29, Stubb's meditation on Ahab's insult raises questions about the status and effect of language. At first Stubb meditates on Ahab's "queer" behavior and how his captain is "full of riddles" (111, 112). As if he does not fully comprehend what Ahab said, Stubb's thoughts then wander to the actual insult: "But how's that? didn't he call me a dog? blazes! he called me ten times a donkey, and piled a lot of jackasses on top of *that!*" (112). But it is Stubb's next reflective sentence that alerts readers that Melville is aware of the volatility of language: "He [Ahab] might as well have kicked me, and done with it. Maybe he *did* kick me, and I didn't observe it, I was so taken all aback with his brow, somehow" (ibid.).

In this passage, Stubb acknowledges he is confused as to whether Ahab actually physically kicked him; he is unsure whether Ahab injured him verbally or corporeally. Stubb considers Ahab's insult to be an action because it has a performative effect—it carries a force within it and constitutes Stubb as an injured party. Because Ahab's overpowering personality so captures Stubb's attention, Stubb wonders if by being taken "aback with his [Ahab's] brow," he misunderstands whether Ahab kicked or slandered. But how could Stubb confuse bodily harm with verbal harm? Shouldn't he know if he had been assaulted or not? If Ahab's words can be seen as having an injurious effect tantamount to a physical kick, then what is the status of words in the face of Stubb's uncertainty about how to interpret language? Is Stubb hyperbolically complaining about Ahab's slur or, by failing to understand his captain's meaning, is Stubb resisting being interpellated into Ahab's ideological structure?

In her Nobel Prize acceptance speech in 1993, Toni Morrison claimed, "Oppressive language does more than represent violence; it is violence." Stubb's confusion about Ahab's insult, then, demonstrates the power of performative speech—that is, speech that performs an action rather than describing or remarking upon a situation. There is no gap of time between pronouncing and acting, which means "the saying is itself the doing, and that they are one another simultaneously" (Butler 17). In other words, Stubb finds his captain's words so menacing because Ahab does not merely utter injurious words but hurls them with such force that Stubb thinks he has been bodily attacked. Ahab's affront shows readers how to do things with words, or how words can strike hard enough to be mistaken for physical blows.

In this scene, language reveals itself to be a force; words not only cause emotional distress but can themselves constitute action powerful enough to deliver a kick. Ahab's anger results in assaultive language that deals a corporeal blow. Speech act theory relies on Austin's distinctions between "perlocutionary" speech and "illocutionary" speech. Perlocutionary speech is constative speech that reports or describes the world or that can lead to an action. For example, when your mother says, "I am thirsty," she is stating a fact, but her words make you get up and pour her a glass of water. Illocutionary speech, however, erodes the distinction between word and action; it is that which performs an action. For example, the cleric who says, "I now pronounce you husband and wife," is not reporting an event but creating and substantiating a litigable identity through words.

Another way of distinguishing between illocutionary and perlocutionary utterances is to see that the "illocutionary speech act is itself the deed that it effects; the perlocutionary merely lead to certain effects" (Butler 3). As another example from *Moby-Dick,* when in chapter 37 Captain Ahab says, "I now prophecy that I will dismember my dismemberer" (143), he enacts the prophecy as he utters it; the saying is the doing. If Stubb claims to be injured by language, then, following Judith Butler, we can "ascribe an agency to language, a power to injure, and position ourselves as the objects of its injurious trajectory" (1). Butler goes on to write that "linguistic injury appears to be the effect not only of the words by which one is addressed but the mode of address itself, a mode—a disposition or conventional bearing—that interpellates and constitutes a subject" (2). Butler argues that injurious language may appear "to fix or paralyze the one it hails, but it may also produce an unexpected and enabling response" (ibid.). The linguistic injury that Ahab levels upon Stubb can be seen as a moment that reinscribes and clarifies the arrangement of power between the two men. Ahab performatively utters an injury that enacts a structure of dominance that sends Stubb, dog-like with his tail between his legs, whimpering back to his kennel.

Stubb feels particularly injured because Ahab calls him a dog, "ten times a donkey, and a mule, and an ass" (111). Had Queequeg or Flask used those same words against Stubb, it is likely Stubb would not have taken offense because his mates do not hold the same position of authority. In order for the utterance to have what Austin terms a "felicitous" effect, it must be leveled by someone in power. As Rae Langton argues, "The authoritative role of the speaker imbues the utterance with a force that would be absent were it made by someone who did not occupy that role" (304). Since Ahab is the authority figure in the scene, his words meet the felicity condition so that his insult is an illocution that authoritatively ranks Stubb as inferior, subordinates Stubb's request to Ahab's will, and constitutes an injury.

Ahab no doubt chooses those animal names to level as an insult because of their history as debased comparisons. Those animal names, when used as slurs, conjure a "force of reiterated convention" (Butler 33). Had Ahab said to Stubb, "down, gazelle, and kennel" or "down, whale, and kennel," no injury would have resulted. The utterance would have been infelicitous or a misfire. In choosing *dog, donkey,* and *ass,* Ahab cites by accessing a rich context that assigns meaning, and thus injury. The felicity, or success, of Ahab's insult relies on the citational nature of language.

Being called a dog or being likened to a donkey or ass inaugurates Stubb into a structure of dominance that privileges Ahab. Since, according to Butler, that interpellation "is an act of speech whose 'content' is neither true nor false," and "its purpose is to indicate and establish a subject in subjection" (33–34), Ahab's insult thereby wounds Stubb, even though Ahab is not the inventor or originator of the injurious language (Ahab did not invent using *dog* as an insult; he is merely citing its slanderous connotation). In citing, Ahab makes "linguistic community" (Butler 52) with previous users of that slur. The insult is so efficacious because of the "invocation of convention," despite Ahab's intention or level of awareness of his utterance's effect. Ahab likely did not realize, and did not care about, the full impact or force his words would have, but because of the iterability of injurious language and the "citational character of speech" (Butler 39), his insult hits hard.

Given the structure of dominance inaugurated by linguistic injury, it can be difficult to level resistance against the authoritative nature of persecutory language. How can one who is wounded by words strike back? How can the performativity of a speech act be turned against the performative injury? It is extremely difficult to use injurious language without reenacting the injury (Butler 14). For example, to litigate against racist language, the damaging epithet and hurt must be repeated and thus relived. However, to counter the injurious label of *queer,* the gay community has positively reclaimed and reappropriated that term, thereby reassigning it an affirmative value. *Queer* thus repeats a historically damaging slur without reenacting the damage. I want to discuss the way that Stubb devises a completely different strategy for countering the effects of Ahab's insult. Stubb does not reappropriate the word *dog* nor rehabilitate the terms *donkey* and *ass.* He does not cite harmful language against itself. Instead, Melville enacts a different strategy of resistance in order to disarm persecutory language. It is this linguistic strategy that I want to explore next.

Maimed Body, Maimed Language

In chapter 31, Stubb reports a strange dream to Flask: "You know the old man's ivory leg, well I dreamed he kicked me with it; and when I tried to kick back, upon my soul, my little man, I kicked my leg right off!" (113).[3] Obviously identifying himself with Ahab's own missing leg, Stubb then tells Flask that in his dream he imagined Ahab as a pyramid that he kept kicking at. Eventually, Stubb's kicking brings about the realization that Ahab's rudeness "was not much of an insult, that kick from Ahab. 'Why,' thinks I, 'what's the row? It's not a real leg, only a false leg.' And there's a mighty difference between a living thump and a dead thump. That's what makes a blow from the hand, Flask, fifty times more savage to bear than a blow from a cane. The living member—that makes the living insult, my little man."

Stubb concludes that Ahab's kick does not injure as much as it could because the captain kicks with a false leg. Stubb differentiates between the injurious potential of a "living thump and a dead thump"—referring to Ahab's kick with a real leg as opposed to an artificial one—and thus claims that a blow from "a living member" wounds more than a blow from a metonymic substitute. By interpreting the "kick" from a prosthetic as less harmful than that from an original, Stubb perceives Ahab's physical force with a maimed leg as an artificial, and thus inferior, substitute for a real kick.

When Stubb ruminates on Ahab's false leg, we see Melville theorizing the relationship between language and action. By dwelling on the idea of Ahab's prosthesis, Stubb becomes an insightful philosopher about maimed language and action as he finds a way to demote injurious speech when it is uttered from a mutilated source. The result is that Ahab, instead of being seen as an all-powerful orator who assigns hurtful authority to language, becomes a speaker manqué, a man whose words stand as a downgraded substitute for action just as his peg leg disables his ability to act with as much force as if his leg were real. I want to argue that, rather than having Stubb re-cite or reclaim Ahab's animal insults against themselves as a strategic way to deactivate the harmful utterances, Melville instead redirects Stubb's resistance to Ahab's disability in order to disarm the very status of injurious language itself.

Ahab's kick is not the first instance of a booting in the novel. Stubb's questions to himself about Ahab's kick refer back to the theme of kicking in the novel's opening scenes. In the first chapter, for example, Ishmael ponders the "thump and punch" (21) that sea captains may give him and expands upon this potential for injury by considering that "everybody else is one way or other served in much the same way—either in a physical or metaphysical point of view" (ibid.). Stubb's uncertainty about his being injured by Ahab is therefore coterminous with the corporeal or verbal ("physical or metaphysical") "thump and punch" theme so universally felt. If life is a series of kicks, whether felt bodily or emotionally, then Melville explores the way such kicks are experienced linguistically.[4]

Ishmael also reports, "I felt a sudden sharp poke in my rear, and turning round, was horrified at the apparition of Captain Peleg in the act of withdrawing his leg from my immediate vicinity. That was my first kick" (94). Peleg continues to move about the ship "here and there using his leg very freely" (95), suggesting that he does not end his disciplinary kicking spree. Paul Royster interprets this scene as demonstrative of Ishmael's defensive strategy that allows him to avoid being embarrassed or demeaned by his working-class position. By linking Peleg's kick to the "universal thump and bump," Ishmael thus "transforms this striking example of class relations (owner/employee) into an illustration of higher democracy," so that whaling is "an occupation representative of the universal human condition, even if this blurs the distinction between industrial discipline and human equality" (314). By universalizing abusive workplace kicks, Ishmael rationalizes his underling status.

Yet we must remember that Ahab verbally, not bodily, assaults Stubb. Since Ahab "kicks" with his words, Stubb thus erases the distinction between word and action. But, if this kick from a prosthesis harms less than one from an original, then Ahab's verbal insult, mistaken for a kick, is maimed. Stubb mistakes Ahab's insult for a kick, but the kick proves to be downgraded because it is delivered with an artificial substitute; likewise, the novel suggests that a verbal kick might function similarly, with the original language delivering the kick also proving to be ineffective. The power of Ahab's performative utterance to enact an injury, while still hitting its mark (felicitous in Austin's term), is lessened because Stubb uses his own language to rationalize, demote, and thus "arrest the force" (Butler 1) of Ahab's invective.

Stubb at first understands and subscribes to the conventions surrounding Ahab's insult, which produced the initial injury. However, by altering the convention so that Ahab's strike is seen as but prosthetic, Stubb reclaims a position of agency within the circuit of performativity. Thus, Stubb exercises "the force of language even as [he] seek[s] to counter its force" (Butler 1). Ahab's injurious speech stands as a maimed form of language next to Stubb's verbally dextrous capacity to convert Ahab's physical disability into a linguistic disability. Stubb diminishes Ahab's capacity "to do things with words" because he recognizes the words themselves derive from a maimed origin.

Prosthesis

Stubb's claim that Ahab's prosthetic leg fails to deliver a "living insult" points out the arbitrary connection between signifier and signified. On the one hand we can see Ahab's verbal insult as performative speech because of the way it enacts an injury. On the other hand, Stubb's analysis of the prosthetic limb's lessened effect instead demonstrates language to be a sign that deceives, conceals, or performs a prosthesis. As David Mitchell points out, the close association between disability and moral flaw is not necessarily instinctive but is facilitated by what he calls the "language of prosthesis." Drawing upon David Wills's book *Prosthesis,* Mitchell argues that "the prosthetic relation between natural and artificial—the attempt to simulate a living appendage with a wooden or inorganic substitute—

serves as the proper metaphor for the workings of language itself. . . . For Wills, the word is an artificial extension of the body seeking to capture an elusive essence: 'Language inaugurates a structure of the prosthetic when the first word projects itself from the body into materiality'" (358).

Through Stubb's interpretation of Ahab's insult as a kick, Melville theorizes language as "an artificial extension of the body seeking to capture an elusive essence" (Mitchell 358). Language therefore "inaugurates a structure of the prosthetic" the moment it is uttered. Mitchell further claims that "language disguises its inability to represent anything once and for all, and thus, the sign acts as an elaborate system of deception. The sign's ability to conceal that the relation of signifier and signified is a thoroughly artificial one seeks to perform a prosthesis upon the 'Real'" (358). By taking a whalebone prosthesis and using it to observe the lessened efficacy of a verbal kick, Melville simultaneously enacts and questions the performative effect of language. However, the performative power of language shows that language is not artificial—it wounds and strikes.

After recasting Ahab's prosthetic kick as less powerful, Stubb then further rationalizes to himself Ahab's behavior by likening the kick to an ennobling honor: "Captain Ahab kicked ye, didn't he? . . . it wasn't a common pitch pine leg he kicked with, was it? No, you were kicked by a great man, and with a beautiful ivory leg, Stubb. It's an honor. . . . In old England the greatest lords think it great glory to be slapped by a queen, and made garter-knights of; but, be *your* boast, Stubb, that ye were kicked by old Ahab, and made a wise man of. Remember what I say; *be* kicked by him; account his kicks honors; and on no account kick back" (114). Here Stubb arrests the force of an illocutionary utterance by inverting the insult into an honor. He inflates what was debased and invites further glory through continued kicks of honor.

At this point I want to examine further Stubb's conviction that Ahab had not really injured him deeply, either in body or speech, because Ahab strikes with an artificial substitute for something real and missing. Mitchell argues that "Ahab's disability proves recalcitrant to the linguistic ambiguity that destabilizes the truth-telling systems of human knowledge addressed in the novel" (355). In other words, although *Moby-Dick* roils with ambivalent symbols and unsolvable philosophical issues, Ahab's narrativized bodily injury and its effect on his personality appear clear and unequivocal because Melville goes to great lengths to connect the whale's attack to Ahab's yearning for vengeance. For example, Melville writes that after the whale attack, Ahab's "torn body and gashed soul bled into one another; and so interfusing, made him mad" (156). Because of this direct causal link between injury and revenge, Ahab's dismasting resists multiple possibilities for interpretation amidst the novel's sea of "linguistic ambiguity."[5]

Ahab can be situated in a literary aesthetic of what Mitchell terms "dire bodies," which he describes as "a means of artistic characterization" that "allowed authors to visually privilege something amiss or 'tragically flawed' in the very biology of an embodied character" (362). For example, when Ahab proclaims, "I am the Fates' lieutenant; I act under orders" (418), he asserts that he has no free will but acts under order of a higher power. Ahab thus reinforces how "physical disability becomes synonymous in the text with the tragedy of a deterministic fate" (364). The damaged body is perceived as having a predetermined script written for it.

Ahab's manic desire for revenge is easy for the reader to recognize and believe, according to Mitchell, because Ahab's disfigurement serves as literary shorthand for a flawed character. His artificial leg, like Richard III's or Quasimodo's hunched back, Simon Legree's bullet-shaped head, the deformities of Frankenstein's monster, or Oedipus's blindness, immediately signals to the reader a certain way to read or classify his character and destiny. Some novels may feature disability to raise sympathy (for example, Tiny Tim in Charles Dickens's *A Christmas Carol,* the blind Mr. Rochester in Charlotte Brontë's *Jane Eyre,* perhaps even wrongly sized Gulliver in Jonathan Swift's *Gulliver's Travels*). In chapter 106, Ahab is described as having lain crumpled on the ground as a pathetic cripple, but this scene of pity does not rehabilitate Ahab as a heartwarming character: "He had been found one night lying prone upon the ground, and insensible; by some unknown, and seemingly inexplicable, unimaginable casualty, his ivory limb having been so violently displaced, that it had stake-wise smitten, and all but pierced his groin" (355). No character sees Ahab lying thus and feels pity or empathy for him; Ahab's crippled nature demonizes, rather than humanizes, him.

Since an outward physical defect historically has signaled an inward moral defect, when Ahab rues, "I feel strained, half stranded, as ropes that tow dismasted frigates in a gale" (418), his lament demonstrates, according to Mitchell, that "this sense of being simultaneously immobilized and towed by another vessel proffers a vision of the disabled body firmly yoked to the tragically specular logic of nineteenth-century discourses on physical difference. Disability conjures up a ubiquitous series of associations between corrupted exterior and contaminated interior. The pairing is no more *natural* or aesthetically arresting than a truncated leg buttressed by a whale-bone shaft, but the language of prosthesis would make it seem so" (365). To demonstrate this pairing between disability and interiority, Melville shows us Ahab bemoaning his lack: In chapter 36 Ahab laments his "dead stump" that makes him a "poor pegging lubber" (139). In chapter 37, he refers to his proxy leg as if it were some geometric shape rather than a body part: "my one cogged circle" (143). Further, in chapter 108, the carpenter mutters that Ahab's disability means he has a "stick of whale's jaw-bone for a wife" (361), instead of a loving confidante.

In turn, in the same chapter Ahab refers to the ship's carpenter as "manmaker" (359), a name that reduces and aligns Ahab's manhood to prosthesis and recognizes that any rescue from his shattered masculinity rests on another man's handiwork in crafting a substitute limb. Ahab fantasizes about what a perfectly forged and complete man would look like: "I'll order a complete man after a desirable pattern. Imprimis, fifty feet high in his socks; then, chest modelled after the Thames Tunnel; then, legs with roots to 'em, to stay in one place; then, arms three feet through the wrist; no heart at all, brass forehead, and about a quarter of an acre of fine brains; and let me see—shall I order eyes to see outwards? No, but put a sky-light on top of his head to illuminate inwards" (ibid.). But this fantasy of machine perfection and a whole body does not last long. Cast down, Ahab agonizes: "Oh, Life! Here I am, proud as Greek god, and yet standing debtor to this blockhead for a bone to stand on! Cursed be that mortal inter-indebtedness which will not do away with ledgers. I would be free as air; and I'm down in the whole world's books" (360). Ahab returns to a lament for his lack of completeness, his lack of wholeness, and his need to rely on surrogacy.

The mates' discussion of Ahab's kick also carries distinct homosexual undertones, which further imbue Ahab's act with an aura of substitution and supposed lack of full masculine potency. In addition to the "wadding" mentioned earlier, when Stubb downplays Ahab's kick, he says that Ahab gave him "only a playful cudgelling—in fact, only a whaleboning that he gave me" (113). Further, Stubb diminishes Ahab's power by diminishing the size of Ahab's stick; Stubb describes Ahab's leg as "a small sort of end

. . . this insult is whittled down to a point only" (ibid.). In his dream that he reports to Flask, Stubb says that while he was stubbing his toe against the pyramidal Ahab, an old merman appeared to him and demanded to know Stubb's identity.[6] Angered, Stubb asks the merman if he would like a kick. In the dream, the old merman turns his buttocks to Stubb, bends over, and pushes away the seaweed he uses to cover his back end. Stubb reports that "his stern was stuck full of marlinspikes, with the points out. Says I, on second thoughts, 'I guess I won't kick you, old fellow'" (114). The merman calls Stubb "wise" and chews his gums "like a chimney hag" (ibid.). This curious dream of crossing gender and species, laden with homosexual acts, further draws out Stubb's concern with Ahab's kick. By piling homosexuality and bestiality onto the theme of the kick, Melville calls into question the link between sexuality and complete masculinity, and thus further draws attention to his interest in disability and substitution, whether of manhood or language.

Perhaps Ahab's interest in the prosthetic can be most cogently seen in the famous "little lower layer" soliloquy referenced above. In it, Ahab describes how he wants to "strike through the mask" (140) to try to access meaning. This phrase tidily encapsulates Ahab's conflation of violence and prosthesis. A mask is artifice—it is a prosthetic, a false face, a dissembling facade, used to substitute for the actor's own face in order to compensate for the inabilities or shortcomings of the actor to simulate or represent. Ahab's desire to "strike through" the artifice underscores his desire to do violence to the prosthetic, which echoes the violent kick from the prosthetic limb. His repeated attempts to strike through show that his "vulnerability to language [is] a consequence of [his] being constituted within its terms" (Butler 2). Melville linguistically conjoins prosthesis with force to show the limitations of a proxy. Ahab is unable to strike through the mask, and Stubb arrests the force of Ahab's linguistically injurious strike by linking it to prosthesis.

As the ship's authority, Ahab represents centralized power; thus, when Stubb finds a way to deflect Ahab's linguistic agency, Stubb challenges institutional, regulated power. By meditating on Ahab's disability, Stubb aestheticizes his captain's false leg and makes it an object to be contemplated and an index of action manqué. Ahab's maimed leg becomes a "textual object" to be read and interpreted as a step removed from its "conventional force and meaning" (Butler 99–100). The tethering of Ahab's body to a rhetoric of physical incapacity or substitution links his maimed body to a maimed language. The surrogacy of his limb diminishes the verbal lashing Ahab gives Stubb, which Stubb confuses for a physical kick from a proxy source. Stubb's canny ability to recast the performativity of Ahab's illocutionary subordination and diminish the injury thus highlights strategic ways to resist the force of linguistic wounding and suggests the possibility of an inherently prosthetic nature to language itself.

CONCLUSION

The Right Words and National Standing

When Barack Obama stood with his right hand raised at his swearing-in ceremony on 20 January 2009, he engaged in an act of performative speech that would transform him from president-elect to president: repeating after Chief Justice John Roberts, he intoned, "I, Barack Hussein Obama, do solemnly swear . . ." However, Roberts then mixed up his administration of the words of the oath of office. Instead of stating the phrase ". . . that I will faithfully execute the office of president of the United States" for Obama to repeat, Roberts mistakenly rearranged the order and placed "faithfully" as the last word. Consequently, Obama also stumbled over the recitation of the oath. Roberts then restated the phrase correctly, but Obama repeated back Roberts' original, incorrect version. Some officials believed that Obama's performative utterance of the entire oath constituted a misfire or misexecution. Since Obama said the right words in the right situation but in the wrong order, he failed to swear felicitously. Some worried that since Obama did not utter the constitutionally mandated speech act, he did not properly become president. To ensure that Obama would indeed become president, a second administration of the oath of office occurred the following day in the White House Map Room. Roberts stated, and Obama repeated, the oath without flaws.

I am fascinated by the way that the assumption of power is predicated on a performative speech act such that the change of power cannot be accomplished if one word is out of order. To prevent detractors from arguing that Obama's infelicitous utterance would negate his becoming commander in chief, he re-performed the oath. It is also fascinating that Chief Justice Roberts also said the right words of the oath in the right order but did not himself become president. For the conditions of the mantle of power to shift, all in the United States had to understand and agree to the fact that both Roberts and Obama would utter the same words but that only the latter would become president.

Similarly, on 20 April 2013, Queen Beatrix of the Netherlands abdicated her throne in favor of her son Willem Alexander. Although she announced her intentions to resign in January 2013, that information alone did not suffice as a resignation. Her son could not become king just by Beatrix stating she would like to pass the monarchy to Willem. To relinquish her thirty-three-year rule officially, she had to sign papers of abdication in a ceremony. The statement she signed read, "I declare that I hereby step down from the monarchy of the Kingdom of the Netherlands, that the monarchy from this moment on is transferred to my eldest son and heir Willem-Alexander, Prince of Orange, in accordance with the statutes and the constitution of the Kingdom of the Netherlands." The performativity of "I declare" and the force of her signature (as discussed in chapter 2) created the condition of abdication and inaugurated the situation of her son becoming king. The moment before she signed the document, her title was Queen Beatrix. The moment she put pen to document, she became Princess Beatrix. Willem-Alexander's official swearing in ceremony as king occurred separately before a joint session of the Dutch parliament at Nieuwe Kerk, a decommissioned church in Amsterdam.

My fascination with the performativity of words to effect change on a national level resonates with me on a personal level. When I became a citizen of Canada, I gathered in a Toronto government office with hundreds of people from scores of nations. For most, the ceremony marked the culmination of years of dreaming to attain citizenship in a western democracy. Some people came dressed up in fancy clothes for this all-important event. I wore jeans and carried an infant in my arms who was legally entitled to Canadian citizenship because of his father. All of us partaking in the ceremony repeated the oath, "I swear [or affirm] that I will be faithful and bear true allegiance to Her Majesty Queen Elizabeth II, Queen of Canada, Her Heirs and Successors, and that I will faithfully observe the laws of Canada and fulfill my duties as a Canadian citizen." Before stating that pledge, we were a motley collection of immigrants, political refugees, trailing spouses, asylum seekers, and others. Less than a minute later, after performatively uttering the oath, we became Canadians.

But the man next to me remained mysteriously silent. He actually did not move his lips during the recitation of the oath. Yet he became a citizen. And I must confess a hesitation on my part. Although I did hold the intention of observing Canada's laws, I did not really believe my words when I said I would bear allegiance to the Queen. Citizens of the United States tend to look a bit askance at the role of the Queen and the royal family, and I as well could not take seriously an oath of fidelity to a monarch. Was my performative utterance therefore felicitous? Did I commit a misexecution or misfire? According to Canadian officials, however, the silent man and I both fulfilled our obligations. We received our legal papers and dispersed into the sunny Toronto afternoon.

Antebellum writers proved in many ways to be theorists of performative speech *avant la lettre*. The importance of the performative ramifies to many other fields besides literary studies. Austin first theorized about performatives in his field of analytic philosophy and the philosophy of language, and scholars have made use of the performative in such varied fields as cultural theory, anthropology, and cognitive science. I imagine my study of the performativity of language in the antebellum period as just one entry in a new vein of scholarship; I invite scholars to extend this inquiry into other literary fields and periods.

The chapters in this book respond to each other by meditating on the power of words and the sometimes ambivalent status of linguistic power. The first two chapters problematize the binding nature of the promise, the temperance pledge, and the signature, and their affinities to ideas of freedom and self-agency. The last three chapters theorize injurious speech. For example, both Hester and Stubb reappropriate injurious language. Hester's appropriation of the *A* compares to Stubbs's reassignment of Ahab's linguistic damage through recourse to Ahab's disability. Although Hawthorne and Melville want to distance readers from the utterers of caustic language, Stowe wants us to sympathize with the one leveling the injury.

Humans connect through language; through the power of words we bind ourselves into communities. Although sometimes we use words constatively, as when describing how antebellum authors strategically deploy performative speech in their published writing, sometimes we use words performatively. I promise.

Notes

Introduction

1. Eve Kosofsky Sedgwick points out potential slippage when a gay marriage is not recognized. Jason Edwards writes that "Sedgwick invites us to think about what it might mean and how it might feel, for queer folk, or people not presently in a dyadic sexual couple recognized by society, to be invited to bear witness to a couple tying a knot that they are unable or unwilling to tie themselves" (8).

2. "According to Searle, the rules governing the making of a request (and of any other illocutionary act) are not regulative but constitutive; that is, they do not regulate an antecedently existing behavior, but define the conditions under which that behavior can be said to occur; if those conditions are unfulfilled, that behavior is either defective or void (some conditions are more centrally constitutive than others); the speaker will have done something (one cannot help but do things with words), but he will not have performed the act in question" (Fish 984).

3. John Searle takes issue with Austin's distinction between locutionary and illocutionary in "Austin on Locutionary and Illocutionary Acts."

4. For an extension of this argument, see Hirsh, "Austin's Ditch," and Derrida, *Limited Inc.*

5. According to Miller, "Iterability is *difference*, that is, an opening within the utterance itself that makes it differ from itself, within itself. Iterability opens a gap within the utterance, but also makes it defer itself, opening up abysses of temporality before and after, in a kind of future anterior. This temporality makes the present never present because it always reaches toward a past that was never present and a future that will never be reached as present" (81).

6. For example, see Gura, "Language and Meaning: An American Tradition," and Roger, "Taking a Perspective." Interesting work has also been done on speech in the early republic. For example, Sandra Gustafson coins the term "the performative semiotic of speech and text," in which "claims to authenticity and relations of power were given form and meaning through the reliance on or freedom from text in oral performance. . . . As a symbolic and performative approach to verbal forms, the performance semiotic provides an important corrective to

the developmental trajectory from orality to literacy that still often dominates histories of language" (xvi–xvii).

7. Other sources important for affect studies include Aldama, *Towards a Cognitive Theory of Narrative Acts;* Hoffman, *Empathy and Moral Development;* and Hogan, *Affective Narratology.*

8. The bibliography on speech act theory is extensive. In addition to Austin and Butler, I have found most helpful: Kent Bach and Robert M. Harnish's "How Performatives Really Work"; Kenneth Burke's "Words as Deed"; Stanley Cavell's "Austin and Examples" (included in *The Claim of Reason*); Jaques Derrida's "Signature Event Context" (included in *Limited Inc*); Stanley Fish's "How to Do Things with Austin and Searle"; Barbara Johnson's "Poetry and Performative Language"; J. Hillis Miller's *Speech Acts in Literature;* Sandy Petrey's *Speech Acts and Literary Theory;* Mary Louis Pratt's *Toward a Speech-Act Theory of Literary Discourse;* Searle's *Speech Acts;* and Richard van Oort's "Performative-Constative Revisited." Two recent volumes that address the European tradition are Angela Estherhammer's *The Romantic Performative* and Mauro Senatore's edited volume *Performatives After Deconstruction.*

---

1. Slave Promises and the Temperance Pledge

1. Cindy Weinstein has persuasively argued why the marriage vow itself can be very fraught, especially in sentimental fiction and especially coming from the pen of E.D.E.N. Southworth. Weinstein rightfully questions how the "I do" "is always potentially tainted by its insecure relation to the person saying it (has it been said before?) and the person asking them both to say it (is the woman being set up by a couple of devious men?)" ("What did you mean" 46). According to Weinstein, "Southworth thinks of the vow as a quite complicated speech act, which contains within it a possible gap between the speaker's intention and her or his utterance, a gap between the time the vow is uttered and the solemnizing of that vow, and the difference between a vow made in public and a vow kept private" (48). Thus, she concludes, "the words 'I do' are necessary but not sufficient to make a marriage binding" (49). I will not address wedding vows because they are litigable; hence, according to Weinstein, documents and certificates of marriage that buttress the slippage of vows play a central role in Southworth novels.

2. Harriet Jacobs, in *Incidents in the Life of a Slave Girl,* presents many examples of promises made between master and slave—promises of liberation, promises of fair treatment, and promises made by slaves to behave or to reveal information about rebellion. Slaves also make promises to one another; for example, Jacobs promises her grandmother she will try to endure Dr. Flint's humiliations. Jacobs herself, in a direct address to the reader in the tenth chapter, says that writing of her humiliation "pains me to tell you of it; but I have promised to tell you the truth, and I will do it honestly, let it cost me what it may" (83).

3. Thoreau and Emerson, for example, disdained the literary annual, especially with its ornate engravings. In his journal in April 1852, Emerson wrote "The Illustrations in modern books mark the decline of art. 'Tis the dramdrinking of the eye, & candy for food; as whales & horses & elephants, produced on the stage, show decline of drama" (quoted in Lehuu 77). Poe, on the other hand, wanted to be included in literary annuals; in an 1829 letter to Cary and Lea, publishers of the *Atlantic Souvenir,* Poe wrote, "I know of nothing which could give me greater pleasure than to see any of my productions, in so becoming a dress and in such good society as 'The Souvenir' would ensure them" (Lehuu 77).

4. The other engraving is for "Ode" by Reverend John Pierpont, which commemorates the 1851 Boston kidnapping of Thomas Sims, a fugitive slave. The engraving shows two male slaves and one slave woman clutching her baby, being whipped or beaten as well-dressed white men look on while petting a hunting dog (81).

5. It was not uncommon for illustrations to be chosen first, and stories or contributions to be crafted based on the picture. According to Isabel Lehuu, "gift-books' images were not random illustrations. In fact, the adjoined text was usually ordered by the editor for the purpose of providing an appropriate commentary for a previously selected engraving" (96). Similarly, Cynthia Patterson writes that publishers engaged in the practice of "first commissioning engravings for the illustrated periodicals, and then soliciting popular writers to contribute literary matter to explicate the engravings" (136). Since it is unlikely Reverend Samuel May invented the story in "The Heroic Slave-Woman" about his friend Edward Abdy, a known English attorney, the engraving that accompanies the story was either commissioned specifically for *Autographs for Freedom* or was recycled from some other source. Since the engraving follows the scene from "The Heroic Slave-Woman" so closely, it seems reasonable to assume that Douglass and Griffiths saw something in the story that deemed it worthy or attractive enough to be illustrated. Such canonical authors as Hawthorne and Poe "depended on the success of printed formats that owed their success to engravings, fashion plates, and other illustrations" (McGill 183).

6. Some cities boasted of many Washingtonian groups. For example, Amherst, Massachusetts, had enough interest to support the Washington Total Abstinence Society of North Amherst, the South Amherst Washingtonian Total Abstinence Society, and the Amherst West Center Total Abstinence Society. See Mitchell, "Ardent Spirits," 98.

7. For more on the temperance movement, see Reynolds, *Beneath the American Renaissance;* and Reynolds and Rosenthal, introduction to *The Serpent in the Cup: Temperance in American Literature,* 1–10. Amanda Claybaugh points out that Dickens began his career by mocking temperance reform in *Sketches by Box* (1836) and *The Pickwick Papers* (1836–37) (8).

8. Michael R. Booth details a similar plot structure in nineteenth-century melo-

drama. He describes the typical temperance drama plot as follows: "The first act exhibits a young married couple with children, whose happiness is marred only by the husband's tendency to reach for the bottle. Encouraged by the inevitable melodramatic villain with designs on wife and property, or both, he falls deeper into the cesspool of alcohol, turns nasty to his wife, and wanders irresponsibly as a drunken vagrant far from home. . . . At the last possible moment, the erring husband either regains his senses, swears off liquor forever, and returns a new man to his joyful family, or, more frequently, a temperance spokesman appears as *deus ex machina* to save him. After surviving dreadful attacks of *delirium tremens*, the hero signs the pledge and is rewarded by unexpected wealth, the imprisonment of the villain, a devotion to the cause of temperance, and renewed tenderness from his ever-faithful, ever-suffering wife" (207).

9. Today's International Order of Good Templars retains a pledge of temperance in its membership application. Those who want to join must pledge "to lead a life free from the use of alcohol and other nonmedical use of dependence producing drugs and to promote public acceptance of this principle." See http://www.iogt.org/wp-content/uploads/2011/09/Application-for-ind-membership-in-IOGT-I.pdf.

10. Sigourney goes on to write that the reformed drunk "may not be able to answer the ingenious and plausible arguments, with which his tempters assail him; but he falls back with confidence and safety upon his pledge, as upon a conclusion to which he arrived, in a season more propitious than the present, for determining his duty. And now, although the peril of the crisis be so great, as to strip him of every other resource and every other means of escape, yet here, in the temperance pledge is that 'last plank' which saves him. There is another consideration, showing the value of the pledge to the reformed drunkard. . . . If it had not other name to it than his own, it might and probably would avail him little. But his respectable neighbors, and hundreds of thousands of the wise and good all over the land, have honored it with their names; and he feels that he stands in their strength" (41).

11. I will return to Derrida more in chapter 2 in my discussion of Fanny Fern and the signature. For more on citation and iteration, see Halion, "Parasitic Speech Acts."

12. See David S. Reynolds, "Black Cats and Delirium Tremens," in Reynolds and Rosenthal, *The Serpent in the Cup*, 50.

13. For an insightful essay that reads Tom as a typical drunkard's wife in a temperance story, see Cordell, "Enslaving you, body and soul."

14. See Jack S. Blocker's *American Temperance Movements* for the way the Sons of Temperance, an outgrowth of the Washingtonians, in 1842 "adopted a policy of secrecy to remove the liability of public exposure from both the organization and its individual members" (48).

15. According to Carole Lynn Stewart, William Wells Brown, for example, "criticizes [temperance reformer John B.] Gough's lowbrow exploitation of emotion and sympathy, which he uses to move the audience to tears with him and thereby convert them to the pledge" (11).

2. Theorizing the Signature in Fanny Fern's *Ruth Hall*

1. Following Fern's preference as to how she wished to be represented, I will use the name Fanny Fern in this essay to refer to Sara Payson Willis Eldredge Farrington Parton.

2. Many American women writers initially became authors in order to earn money. Such women writers include Louisa May Alcott, Augusta Jane Evans, Caroline Howard Gilman, Grace Greenwood, Sarah Josepha Hale, Caroline Hentz, Caroline Kirkland, Maria McIntosh, E.D.E.N. Southworth, Harriet Beecher Stowe, and Susan Warner.

3. Although Lydia Maria Child, Jane Cannon Swisshelm, and Margaret Fuller worked as editors or correspondents (even foreign correspondents), they were never paid to write a regularly appearing newspaper column (Warren, *Independent* 104).

4. Allison Easton points out that Fern often showed sympathy for lower-class women who had to work (224). Fern published her essay "The Working-Girls of New York" under her legal name of Sara P. Parton, possibly to show the personal significance to her of such situations, particularly of women's dependence on male protectors, and the dangers of impoverishment in widowhood.

5. Much of women authors' financial security came from securing copyright. For further analyses of copyright and the emerging market for American women writers, see Douglas, *The Feminization of American Culture;* Baym, *Women's Fiction* and *American Women Writers;* Coultrap-McQuin, *Doing Literary Business;* Homestead, "Every Body Sees the Theft"; and Winship, *American Publishing in the Mid-Nineteenth Century.*

6. Julie Wilhelm offers a different way to read the novel's concern with capitalism, consumption, and expenditure by reading those economic concerns through comical wordplay and humorous stereotypes: "Fern renders the comic a space of resistance by way of its overt, nonproductive consumption of energy. This technique aligns the novel's comical episodes with its sentimental passages: Both modes of writing solicit audience expenditures, one in the form of laughter and the other in the form of affect" (202).

7. In actuality, Fern did use several names before she settled on "Fanny Fern." For example, Joyce Warren details that Fern published an article titled "Thoughts on Dress" in the *Olive Branch* on 19 July 1851 under the name Tabitha, and again on 20 December 1851 under the name Jack Fern. She signed early pieces for the

True Flag with the name Olivia. Warren writes that, "When Fanny Fern first adopted her name, it was as a pseudonym, but, as time passed, she gradually adopted it as her own name. . . . She only used the name Sara Eldredge and later Sara Parton to sign legal documents. It was as if she had made an identity switch. She was no longer Sara Willis Eldredge Farrington, the domestic woman; she was Fanny Fern, the professional woman" (*Independent* 97, 99, 103).

3. The Scarlet *A* as Action

1. I am borrowing these questions from Rae Langton's inquiries into pornographic speech.

2. See Miller, 111, and Derrida, "Declarations of Independence."

3. My reading concurs with Thomas Loebel's: "This letter, then, also has a spirit. The ministers and magistrates intend it as a punishment that will turn Hester's strong-willed heart so that she will speak the name of the father in a triple sense—to name her fellow adulterer, to bend and to employ language in the authoritative confines of speech, and to appeal to the mercy of God" (10–11).

4. Loebel reads the same passage, but is more interested in "antinomianism as a performance of language that 'goes against the law' in its speech and writing by going against the authoritative laws of speech and writing." His essay investigates "the relation between the letter and the spirit as the performance of language" (6).

5. For further elaboration on verdictives and exercitives, see McGowan, 39–43.

6. Korobkin, "The Scarlet Letter of the Law," expands on this point.

7. Similarly, in Stendhal's *The Red and the Black* (1831), Mme de Renal fears that her punishment for committing adultery will be to have to wear a placard announcing her transgression.

4. Verbal Violence in *Uncle Tom's Cabin*

1. For further discussion of pictorial representation of slavery and the performance of subjection, see the first chapter of Wood, *Blind Memory,* as well as the introduction to Hartman, *Scenes of Subjection.*

2. In *Women and Sisters,* Jean Fagan Yellin notes, "Hundreds of images dramatizing the violence related to the institution of slavery—the separation of families, the seizing, branding, selling, and torturing of men, women, and children—appeared in broadsides, newspapers, and books" (5). Her study brilliantly focuses on one image of a slave woman in particular: "Black, half nude, chained, kneeling in supplication—even now she retains her power" (3).

3. For my critical understanding of sentimentalism, I am drawing upon the work of scholars such as Brown, Hendler, Merish, Noble, and Wardley. In addi-

tion, the way I am discussing sentimentalism owes much to Tompkins and to Sanchez-Eppler.

4. Since the word *voodoo* is closely associated with Anglo-American ideas of black magic, many scholars prefer other orthographies, such as vodun, vodou, Vaudoux, vadoun, and vodoum. These many terms, both in Haitian Creole and in French spelling, refer to Haitian belief systems. See Dayan 34n1.

5. I am indebted to Barbara Hochman for discussing this point with me.

6. Sorisio warns that this sentimental assumption can run into trouble when the buying and selling of slaves' fictional representation echoes their physical bodies being marketed, exploited, and sold.

7. Wolstenholme further discusses Eva's curl of hair as a "fetishized object": though it "seems to carry within it its own power, such power manifests itself only as the object is read; and the object might be misread" (90).

8. Linda Grasso intelligently discusses women writers' late nineteenth-century move toward expressing anger. She writes, "The woman writer's frustrated artistry is depicted with controlled yet seething rage. The change is significant, for the more overt expression of anger about the writing woman's status signals a paradigmatic shift in women's imaginative visions. Beginning in the post-bellum period, power struggles between men and women are no longer ameliorated by forgiveness or the belief in the innate goodness of the human heart; arrogant, sadistic, atheistic men are no longer converted through the goodness, patience, and humility of charitable women; there is no longer sustaining hope in a female community organized around an ethos of nurture and care; and there is no longer redemptive power in women's suffering and sacrificing of self. Instead, [Mary E. Wilkins] Freeman and [Constance Fenimore] Woolson decry the waste of the sacrificed female self; they underscore the deadly effects man-made institutions and aesthetic standards have had on the writing woman's sense of self and literary productivity. And they obviously want revenge; the very act of telling the woman's story guarantees that retribution will be done. The culprits are identified; blame is apportioned; and in the end, even though the writing woman's life and work are lost, her dignity remains intact. In this way Freeman and Woolson ennoble their own position as women writers, for their failures and achievements become part of a much larger legacy of thwarted lives, mighty hungers, and unfinished works."

Grasso's ideas about women expressing anger are important when considering assaultive language. My argument differs in that while Grasso discusses anger as emotion, I am discussing language as action—an action of violence.

9. See Gossett for a discussion of Stowe's claim to divine inspiration (93–97).

10. See especially Warhol, Douglas, and Tompkins.

11. African American literary rejoinders to *Uncle Tom's Cabin* include such early examples as Frederick Douglass's *The Heroic Slave* (1853), Harriet E. Wilson's *Our*

Nig (1859), and Martin R. Delaney's *Blake; or the Huts of America* (1861–62), as well as such recent works as Ishmael Reed's *Flight to Canada* (1976) and Alexander's play here discussed.

12. I borrow the term from Martha Cutter's book *Unruly Tongue*.

---

5. Action and Injurious Speech in *Moby-Dick*

1. My argument builds on the work of other language theorists. For example, Nina Baym lays the groundwork in her discussion of the influence of Emerson's theories of language on Melville. John Bryant, in focusing on the "aesthetics of repose" to discuss Melville's humor, similarly discusses how "words can 'originate' (i.e. re-create) but can never *be* the original objects they represent" (6). Philip Gura writes on how such mid-nineteenth-century writers as Melville "established their aesthetic responses to the critical problems in semantics which troubled so many of their contemporaries" (11). Gayle L. Smith argues that "Ishmael's language choices reflect Melville's awareness that the received language is not adequate to his perception of reality" (260).

2. For an excellent overview of the way Stubb has been neglected in critical commentary and why this oversight should be corrected, see Alan Dagovitz, "*Moby-Dick*'s Hidden Philosopher."

3. Christine Stansell discusses the dream as "one extended dream sequence" that "brings not warning or vision but advice and clarification" (247). She discusses Stubb's dream from a post-Freudian perspective but does not attend to speech act theory.

4. See Leverenz, *Manhood and the American Renaissance,* for a discussion of Ahab's craving for dominance set against his craving for being beaten. In Leverenz's view, the impulse to beat others reflects the desire to be beaten.

5. For further reading on theories of Ahab's body, see Larson, "Of Blood and Words."

6. Alan Dagovitz argues that "the kicking represents Stubb's prideful reaction to Ahab's insult, and the initial loss of his leg is a testimony to how pride turns him into the monomaniacal Ahab that he is struggling against" (338). Edward Rosenberry focuses on the dream as symbolically representing Stubb's yielding to Ahab's force.

Bibliography

Abdy, Edward S. *Journal of a Residence and Tour in the United States of North America from April 1833 to October 1834.* 3 vols. London: John Murray, 1835.

Aldama, Fredick Luis, ed. *Towards a Cognitive Theory of Narrative Acts.* Austin: University of Texas Press, 2011.

Alexander, Robert. *I Ain't Yo' Uncle: The New Jack Revisionist Uncle Tom's Cabin.* In *Colored Contradictions: An Anthology of Contemporary African American Plays,* edited by Harry J. Elam Jr. and Robert Alexander, 21–90. New York: Plume, 1996.

Arac, Jonathan. *Huckleberry Finn as Idol and Target: The Functions of Criticism in Our Time.* Madison: University of Wisconsin Press, 1997.

Arthur, Timothy Shay. *The Lights and Shadows of Real Life.* Philadelphia, 1851.

———. *Temperance Tales, or, Six Nights with the Washingtonians.* 2 vols. Philadelphia, 1848.

———. *Ten Nights in a Bar-Room and What I Saw There.* 1854. Bedford, MA: Applewood Books, 2000.

Augst, Thomas. "Temperance, Mass Culture, and the Romance of Experience." *American Literary History* 19.2 (Summer 2007): 297–323.

Austin, J. L. *How to Do Things with Words.* 2nd ed. Edited by J. O. Urmson and Marina Sbisa. Cambridge: Harvard University Press, 1975.

Bach, Kent, and Robert M. Harnish. "How Performatives Really Work: A Reply to Searle." *Linguistics and Philosophy* 15.1 (1992): 93–110.

Baldwin, James. "Everybody's Protest Novel," in Stowe, *Uncle Tom's Cabin,* 532–39.

Bannett, Nina. "'Unrighteous Compact': Louis May Alcott's Resistance to Contracts and Promises in *Moods.*" In *Popular Nineteenth-Century American Women Writers and the Literary Marketplace,* edited by Earl Yarington and Mary De Jong, 329–48. Newcastle, UK: Cambridge Scholars, 2007.

Barnes, Elizabeth. *States of Sympathy: Seduction and Democracy in the American Novel.* New York: Columbia University Press, 1997.

Baughman, Ernest. "Public Confession and *The Scarlet Letter.*" In Nathaniel Hawthorne, *"The Scarlet Letter" and Other Writings,* edited by Seymour Gross, et al., 207–12. New York: Norton, 1988.

Baym, Nina. *American Women Writers and the Work of History, 1790–1860*. New Brunswick: Rutgers University Press, 1995.

———. "Melville's Quarrel with Fiction." *PMLA* 94.5 (October 1979): 909–23.

———. *Women's Fiction: A Guide to Novels by and about Women in America, 1820–1870*. Champaign: University of Illinois Press, 1993.

Bercovitch, Sacvan. *The Office of the Scarlet Letter*. Baltimore: Johns Hopkins University Press, 1991.

Berlant, Lauren. "The Female Woman: Fanny Fern and the Form of Sentiment." *American Literary History* 3.3 (Autumn 1991): 429–54.

Blocker, Jack S. *American Temperance Movements: Cycles of Reform*. Boston: Twayne Publishers, 1989.

Booth, Michael R. "The Drunkard's Progress: Nineteenth-Century Temperance Drama." *The Dalhousie Review* 44.2 (1964): 205–12.

Brickhouse, Anna. "The Writing of Haiti: Pierre Flaubert, Harriet Beecher Stowe, and Beyond." *American Literary History* 13:3 (Fall 2001): 407–44.

Brodhead, Richard H. *The School of Hawthorne*. New York: Oxford University Press, 1986.

———. [Method in *The Scarlet Letter*]. In Nathaniel Hawthorne, *"The Scarlet Letter" and Other Writings*, edited by Seymour Gross, et al., 392–402. New York: Norton, 1988.

Brown, Gillian. *Domestic Individualism: Imagining Self in Nineteenth-Century America*. Berkeley: University California Press, 1990.

Bryant, John. *Melville and Repose: The Rhetoric of Humor in the American Renaissance*. New York: Oxford University Press, 1993.

Burke, Kenneth. "Words as Deed." *Centrum* 3.2 (1975): 147–68.

Butler, Judith. *Excitable Speech: A Politcis of the Performative*. New York: Routledge, 1997.

Castronovo, Russ. "The Antislavery Unconscious: Mesmerism, Vodun, and 'Equality.'" *Mississippi Quarterly* 53.1 (Winter 1999/2000): 41–56.

Cavell, Stanley. *The Claim of Reason*. Oxford: Oxford University Press, 1979.

Christoph, Julie Nelson. "Reconceiving Ethos in Relation to the Personal: Strategies of Placement in Pioneer Women's Writing." *College English* 64.6 (July 2002): 660–79.

Claybaugh, Amanda. *The Novel of Purpose: Literature and Social Reform in the Anglo-American World*. Ithaca: Cornell University Press, 2006.

Coleman, Dawn. "The Unsentimental Woman Preacher of *Uncle Tom's Cabin*." *American Literature* 80.2 (June 2008): 265–92.

Cordell, Ryan C. "'Enslaving you, body and soul': The Uses of Temperance in *Uncle Tom's Cabin* and 'Anti-Tom' Fiction." *Studies in American Fiction* 36.1 (Spring 2008): 3–26.

Coultrap-McQuin, Susan. *Doing Literary Business: American Women Writers in the Nineteenth Century.* Chapel Hill: University of North Carolina Press, 1990.

Crafts, Hannah. *The Bondswoman's Narrative.* Edited by Henry Louis Gates Jr. New York: Warner Books, 2002.

Crain, Patricia. *The Story of A: The Alphabetization of America from "The New England Primer" to "The Scarlet Letter."* Stanford: Stanford University Press, 2002.

Crane, Gregg D. "Dangerous Sentiments: Sympathy, Rights, and Revolution in Stowe's Antislavery Novels." *Nineteenth-Century Literature* 51.2 (September 1996): 176–204.

Culler, Jonathan. *Literary Theory: A Very Short Introduction.* Oxford: Oxford University Press, 2000.

Cutter, Martha. *Unruly Tongue: Identity and Voice in American Women's Writing, 1850–1930.* Jackson: University Press of Mississippi, 2008.

Dagovitz, Alan. "*Moby-Dick*'s Hidden Philosopher: A Second Look At Stubb." *Philosophy and Literature* 32 (2008): 330–46.

Dayan, Joan. "Vodoun: Or, the Voice of the Gods." *Raritan: A Quarterly Review* 10.3 (Winter 1991): 32–57.

De Man, Paul. *Allegories of Reading.* New Haven: Yale University Press, 1979.

Derrida, Jacques. "Declarations of Independence." *New Political Science* 15 (1986): 7–15.

———. *Limited Inc.* Translated by Samuel Weber and Jeffrey Mehlman. Evanston, IL: Northwestern University Press, 1972.

———. *The Post Card: From Socrates to Freud and Beyond.* Translated by Alan Bass. Chicago: University of Chicago Press, 1987.

Diamond, Elin. Introduction to *Performance and Cultural Politics,* edited by Elin Diamond, 1–12. New York: Routledge, 1996.

Dillingham, William B. "Arthur Dimmesdale's Confession." *Studies in the Literary Imagination* 2.1 (1969): 21–26.

Douglas, Ann. *The Feminization of American Culture.* New York: Knopf, 1977.

Douglass, Frederick. "Intemperance and Slavery: An Address Delivered in Cork, Ireland, on October 20, 1845." http://www.yale.edu/glc/archive/1060.htm.

———. *Narrative of the Life of Frederick Douglass: With Related Documents.* Edited by David W. Blight. Boston: Bedford/St. Martin's, 2003.

Dowling, David. "Capital Sentiment: Fanny Fern's Transformation of the Gentleman Publisher's Code." *American Transcendental Quarterly* 22.1 (2008): 347–64.

Duquette, Elizabeth. *Loyal Subjects: Bonds of Nation, Race, and Allegiance in Nineteenth-Century America.* New Brunswick: Rutgers University Press, 2010.

Easton, Allison. "My Banker and I Can Afford to Laugh!: Class and Gender in Fanny Fern and Nathaniel Hawthorne." In *Soft Canons: American Women Writers and Masculine Tradition,* edited by Karen Kilcup, 219–36. Iowa City: University of Iowa Press, 1999.

"Editor's Outlook." *The Chautauquan: A Monthly Magazine* 17 (June 1893): 355.

Edwards, Jason. *Eve Kosofsky Sedgwick.* New York: Routledge, 2008.

Emerson, Ralph Waldo. "Eloquence." In *Collected Works of Ralph Waldo Emerson, Vol. VII: Society and Solitude,* 30–51. Cambridge: Harvard University Press, 2010.

———. "Nature." In *Nature and Selected Essays,* 35–82. Edited by Larzer Ziff. New York: Penguin, 2003.

Estherhammer, Angela. *The Romantic Performative: Language and Action in British and German Romanticism.* Stanford: Stanford University Press, 2000.

["Fascination No Criticism Will Thwart"]. In Melville, *Moby-Dick,* 602–4.

Fern, Fanny. *"Ruth Hall" and Other Writings.* Edited by Joyce Warren. New Brunswick: Rutgers University Press, 1986.

Fessenden, Tracy. "From Romanism to Race: Anglo-American Liberties in *Uncle Tom's Cabin.*" *Prospects* 25 (2000): 229–68.

Fish, Stanley E. "How to Do Things with Austin and Searle: Speech Act Theory and Literary Criticism." *MLN* 91.5 (October 1976): 983–1025.

Frank, Jason. *Constituent Moments: Enacting the People in Postrevolutionary America.* Durham: Duke University Press, 2010.

Garvey, T. Gregory. "Emerson's Political Spirit and the Problem of Language." In *The Emerson Dilemma: Essays on Emerson and Social Reform,* edited by T. Gregory Garvey, 14–34. Athens: University of Georgia Press, 2000.

Gilmore, Michael T. "Hawthorne and the Making of the Middle Class." In Hawthorne, *"The Scarlet Letter" and Other Writings,* 597–614.

———. "*Uncle Tom's Cabin* and the American Renaissance: The Sacramental Aesthetic of Harriet Beecher Stowe." In *The Cambridge Companion to Harriet Beecher Stowe,* edited by Cindy Weinstein, 58–76. New York: Cambridge University Press, 2004.

Gossett, Thomas. *Uncle Tom's Cabin and American Culture.* Dallas: Southern Methodist University Press, 1985.

Grasso, Linda. "'Thwarted Life, Mighty Hunger, Unfinished Work': The Legacy of Nineteenth-Century Women Writing in America." *American Transcendental Quarterly,* 8.2 (June 1994): 97–118.

Gunn, Robert. "'How I Look': Fanny Fern and the Strategy of Pseudonymity." *Legacy* 27.1 (2010): 23–42.

Gura, Phillip. "Language and Meaning: An American Tradition." *American Literature* 53.1 (March 1981): 1–21.

Gustafson, Sandra. *Eloquence is Power: Oratory and Performance in Early America.* Chapel Hill: University of North Carolina Press, 2000.

Halion, Kevin. "Parasitic Speech Acts: Austin, Searle, Derrida." http://www.e
-anglais.com/parasitic_sa.html#pt2a.

Harris, Jennifer. "Marketplace Transactions and Sentimental Currencies in
Fanny Fern's *Ruth Hall*." *American Transcendental Quarterly* 20.1 (March
2006): 343–59.

Harris, Susan K. "Inscribing and Defining: The Many Voices of Fanny Fern's
Ruth Hall." *Style* 22.4 (Winter 1988): 612–27.

Hartman, Saidiya V. *Scenes of Subjection: Terror, Slavery, and Self-Making in
Nineteenth-Century America*. New York: Oxford University Press, 1997.

Hawthorne, Nathaniel. *"The Scarlet Letter" and Other Writings*. Edited by Leland
S. Person, Norton Critical Editions. New York: Norton, 2005.

Hedrick, Joan D. *Harriet Beecher Stowe: A Life*. New York: Oxford University
Press, 1994.

Hendler, Glenn. "Bloated Bodies and Sober Sentiments: Masculinity in 1840s
Temperance Narratives." In *Sentimental Men: Masculinity and the Politics of
Affect in American Culture,* edited by Mary Chapman and Glenn Hendler,
125–48. Berkeley: University of California Press, 1999.

———. "Further Responses to Marianne Noble on Stowe, Sentiment, and Mas-
ochism." *Yale Journal of Criticism* 12.1 (Spring 1999): 145–67.

Hentz, Caroline Lee. "The Drunkard's Daughter." In *Water Drops from Women
Writers: A Temperance Reader,* edited by Carol Mattingly, 92–110. Carbondale:
Southern Illinois University Press, 2001.

Herbert, Christopher. *Culture and Anomie: Ethnographic Imagination in the
Nineteenth Century*. Chicago: University of Chicago Press, 1991.

Hirsh, James. "Austin's Ditch: The Political Necessity and Impossibility of 'Non-
Serious' Speech." Paper presented at the Twentieth World Congress of Philosophy, Boston, August, 1998. http://www.bu.edu/wcp/Papers/Poli/PoliHers.htm.

Hoffman, Martin L. *Empathy and Moral Development*. Cambridge University
Press, 2001.

Hogan, Patrick Colm. *Affective Narratology: The Emotional Structure of Stories*.
Lincoln: University of Nebraska Press, 2011.

Homestead, Melissa J. "'Every Body Sees the Theft': Fanny Fern and Literary
Proprietorship in Antebellum America." *The New England Quarterly* 74.2 (June
2001): 210–37.

Hochman, Barbara. *"Uncle Tom's Cabin* in the *National Era.*" *Book History* 7
(2004): 143–69.

Jacobs, Harriet A. *Incidents in the Life of a Slave Girl*. Edited by Jean Fagin Yellin.
Cambridge: Harvard University Press, 2000.

Johnson, Barbara. "Poetry and Performative Language: Mallarme and Austin."
In *The Critical Difference,* 52–66. Baltimore: Johns Hopkins University Press,
1980.

Kelley, Mary. *Private Woman, Public Stage: Literary Domesticity in Nineteenth-Century America.* Chapel Hill: University of North Carolina Press, 1984.

Kennedy, Randall. *Nigger: The Strange Career of a Troublesome Word.* NY: Pantheon Books, 2002.

Korobkin, Laura. "The Scarlet Letter of the Law: Hawthorne and Criminal Justice." In Hawthorne, *"The Scarlet Letter" and Other Writings,* 426–51.

Langton, Rae. "Speech Acts and Unspeakable Acts." *Philosophy and Public Affairs* 22.4 (Fall 1993): 293–330.

Larson, Doran. "Of Blood and Words: Ahab's Rhetorical Body." *Modern Language Studies* 25.2 (Spring 1995): 18–33.

Lee, Benjamin. *Talking Heads: Language, Metalanguage, and the Semiotics of Subjectivity.* Durham: Duke University Press, 1997.

Lehuu, Isabel. *Carnival on the Page: Popular Print Media in Antebellum America.* Chapel Hill: University of North Carolina Press, 2000.

Lender, Mark Edward, and James Kirby Martin. *Drinking in America: A History.* New York: Free Press, 1982.

Leverenz, David. *Manhood and the American Renaissance.* Ithaca: Cornell University Press, 1989.

Loebel, Thomas. "'A' Confession: How to Avoid Speaking the Name of the Father." *American Quarterly* 59.1 (Spring 2003): 1–29.

Loxley, James. *Performativity.* New York: Routledge, 2007.

MacKinnon, Catherine, and Andrea Dworkin, eds. *In Harm's Way: The Pornography Civil Rights Hearing.* Cambridge: Harvard University Press, 1997.

May, Samuel J. "The Heroic Slave-Woman." In *Autographs for Freedom,* edited by Julia Griffiths, 161–65. Boston: John P. Jewett, 1853.

McGowan, Mary Kate. "On Pornography: MacKinnon, Speech Acts, and 'False' Construction." *Hypatia* 20.3 (Summer 2005): 22–49.

McGill, Meredith L. "Owning Up to Images: Poe, Hawthorne, and Antebellum Gift-Book Publication." In *Iconotropism: Turning Toward Pictures,* edited by Ellen Spolsky, 183–202. Lewisburg: Bucknell University Press, 2004.

Meer, Sarah. *Uncle Tom Mania: Slavery, Minstrelsy, and Transatlantic Culture in the 1850s.* Athens: University of Georgia Press, 2005.

Melville, Herman. *Moby-Dick.* Edited by Hershel Parker and Harrison Hayford, Norton Critical Editions. New York: Norton, 2002.

Merish, Lori. *Sentimental Materialism: Gender, Commodity Culture, and Nineteenth-Century American Literature.* Durham: Duke University Press, 2000.

Miller, J. Hillis. *Speech Acts in Literature.* Stanford: Stanford University Press, 2001.

Millner, Michael. *Fever Reading: Affect and Reading Badly in the Early American Public Sphere.* New Hampshire: University Press of New England, 2012.

Mitchell, David. "The Language of Prosthesis in *Moby-Dick.*" In *Melville "Among the Nations": Proceedings of an International Conference, Volos, Greece, July 2–6, 1997,* edited by Sanford E. Marovitz and A. C. Christodoulou, 355–66. Kent: Kent State University Press, 2001.

Mitchell, Domhnall. "Ardent Spirits: Temperance in Emily Dickinson's Writing." *Emily Dickinson Journal* 15.2 (2006): 95–112.

Morgan, David. *Visual Piety: A History and Theory of Popular Religious Images.* Berkeley: University of California Press, 1998.

Morrison, Toni. Nobel Prize Acceptance Speech. http://www.nobelprize.org/ nobel_prizes/literature/laureates/1993/morrison-lecture.html.

Noble, Marianne. *The Masochistic Pleasures of Sentimental Literature.* Princeton: Princeton University Press, 2000.

Nudelman, Franny. "'Emblem and Product of Sin': The Poisoned Child in *The Scarlet Letter* and Domestic Advice Literature." *Yale Journal of Criticism* 10.1 (1997): 193–213.

Otter, Samuel. "Stowe and Race." In *The Cambridge Companion to Harriet Beecher Stowe,* edited by Cindy Weinstein, 15–38. Cambridge: Cambridge University Press, 2004.

Parsons, Elaine Frantz. *Manhood Lost: Fallen Drunkards and Redeeming Women in the Nineteenth-Century United States.* Baltimore: Johns Hopkins University Press, 2003.

Patterson, Cynthia. "'Illustrations of a Picture': Nineteenth-Century Writers and the Philadelphia Pictorials." *American Periodicals* 19.2 (2009): 136–64.

Petrey, Sandy. *Speech Acts and Literary Theory.* New York: Routledge, 1990.

Pratt, Mary Louis. *Toward a Speech-Act Theory of Literary Discourse.* Bloomington: Indiana University Press, 1977.

Raboteau, Albert. *Slave Religion: The "Invisible Institution" in the Antebellum South.* New York: Oxford University Press, 1978.

Ragussis, Michael. "Silence, Family Discourse, and Fiction in *The Scarlet Letter.*" *ELH* 49.4 (Winter 1982): 863–88.

Raimon, Eve Allegra. *The "Tragic Mulatta" Revisited: Race and Nationalism in Nineteenth-Century Antislavery Fiction.* New Brunswick: Rutgers University Press, 2004.

Rasmussen, Birgit Brander. *Queequeg's Coffin: Indigenous Literacies and Early American Literature.* Durham: Duke University Press, 2012.

Reddy, William M. *The Navigation of Feeling.* Cambridge: Cambridge University Press, 2001.

Reynolds, David S. *Beneath the American Renaissance: The Subversive Imagination in the Age of Emerson and Melville.* Cambridge: Harvard University Press, 1988.

Reynolds, David S., and Debra J. Rosenthal, eds. *The Serpent in the Cup: Temperance in American Literature.* Amherst: University of Massachusetts Press, 1997.

Robbins, Sarah. "Gendering the History of the Antislavery Narrative: Juxtaposing *Uncle Tom's Cabin* and *Benito Cereno, Beloved* and *Middle Passage.*" *American Quarterly* 49.3 (September 1997): 531–73.

Roger, Patricia M. "Taking a Perspective: Hawthorne's Concept of Language and Nineteenth Century Language Theory." *Nineteenth-Century Literature* 51.4 (March 1987): 433–54.

Rose, Henrietta. *Nora Wilmot: A Tale of Temperance and Women's Rights.* Columbus: Osgood and Pearce, 1858.

Rosenberry, Edward. *Melville and the Comic Spirit.* Cambridge: Harvard University Press, 1955.

Royster, Paul. "Melville's Economy of Language." In *Ideology and Classic American Literature,* edited by Sacvan Bercovitch and Myra Jehlen, 313–36. Cambridge: Cambridge University Press, 1986.

Sanchez, Maria C. "Re-Possessing Individualism in Fanny Fern's *Ruth Hall.*" *Arizona Quarterly* 56.4 (Winter 2000): 25–56.

Sanchez-Eppler, Karen. *Touching Liberty: Abolition, Feminism, and the Politics of the Body.* Berkeley: University of California Press, 1997.

Searle, John R. "Austin on Locutionary and Illocutionary Acts." *The Philosophical Review* 77.4 (October 1968): 405–24.

———. "How Performatives Work." *Linguistics and Philosophy* 12.5 (October 1989): 535–58.

———. *Speech Acts: An Essay in the Philosophy of Language.* Cambridge: Cambridge University Press, 1969.

Sedgwick, Eve Kosofsky. *Touching Feeling: Affect, Pedagogy, Performativity.* Durham: Duke University Press, 2003.

Senatore, Mauro, ed. *Performatives After Deconstruction.* London: Bloomsbury, 2013.

Sigourney, Lydia. *The Intemperate and the Reformed.* Boston: Seth Bliss, 1834.

Silverman, Gillian. "Sympathy and Its Vicissitudes." *American Studies* 43.3 (2002): 5–28.

Simms, William Gilmore [attributed to]. ["Grounds for a Writ *de lunatico* against Melville"]. In Melville, *Moby-Dick,* 624–25.

Smith, Gayle L. "The Word and the Thing: *Moby-Dick* and the Limits of Language." *ESQ* 31.4 (1985): 260–71.

Sorisio, Carolyn. "Spectacle of the Body." *Modern Language Studies* 30.1 (2000): 45–66.

Stansell, Christine. "Historic Passion Dreams." *History Workshop Journal* 62 (2006): 241–52.

Starling, Marion Wilson. *The Slave Narrative: Its Place in American History.* Washington, DC: Howard University Press, 1988.

Stewart, Carole Lynn. "A Transnational Temperance Discourse? William Wells

Brown, Creole Civilization, and Temperate Manners." *Journal of Transnational American Studies* 3.1 (2011): 1–25

Stowe, Harriet Beecher. *A Key to Uncle Tom's Cabin*. 1852. Edited by Elizabeth Ammons. New York: Norton, 1994.

———. *Uncle Tom's Cabin*. Edited by Elizabeth Ammons, Norton Critical Editions. New York: Norton, 2010.

Temple, Gale. "A Purchase on Goodness: Fanny Fern, *Ruth Hall*, and Fraught Individualism." *Studies in American Fiction* 31.2 (2003): 131–63.

Thomas, Brook. *American Literary Realism and the Failed Promise of Contract*. Berkeley: University of California Press, 1999.

Thrailkill, Jane. *Affecting Fiction: Mind, Body, and Emotion in American Literary Realism*. Cambridge: Harvard University Press, 2007.

Tompkins, Jane. *Sensational Designs: The Cultural Work of American Fiction, 1790–1860*. Oxford: Oxford University Press, 1985.

Van Oort, Richard. "Performative-Constative Revisited: The Genetics of Austin's Theory of Speech Acts." *Anthropoetics* 2.2 (January 1997). http://www.anthropoetics.ucla.edu/Ap0202/Vano.htm.

Varon, Elizabeth R. *Disunion! The Coming of the American Civil War, 1789–1859*. Chapel Hill: University of North Carolina Press, 2008.

Wardley, Lynn. "Relic, Fetish, Femmage: The Aesthetics of Sentiment in the Work of Stowe." *The Culture of Sentiment: Race, Gender, and Sentimentality in Nineteenth-Century America*, edited by Shirley Samuels, 203–20. New York: Oxford University Press, 1992.

Warhol, Robyn R. *Gendered Interventions: Narrative Discourse in the Victorian Novel*. New Brunswick: Rutgers University Press, 1989.

Warren, Joyce. *Fanny Fern: An Independent Woman*. New Brunswick: Rutgers University Press, 1994.

———. "Fanny Fern, Performative Incivilities, and Rap." *Studies in American Humor* 3.6 (1999): 17–36.

———. Introduction to Fern, *"Ruth Hall" and Other Writings*, ix–xxxix.

Weinstein, Cindy. *Family, Kinship, and Sympathy in Nineteenth-Century American Literature*. Cambridge: Cambridge University Press, 2004.

———. "'What did you mean?': Marriage in E.D.E.N. Southworth's Novels." *Legacy* 27.1 (2010): 43–60.

Weyler, Karen. "Literary Labors and Intellectual Prostitution: Fanny Fern's Defense of Working Women." *South Atlantic Review* 70.2 (2005): 96–131.

Wilheim, Julie. "An Expenditure Saved Is an Expenditure Earned: Fanny Fern's Humoring of the Capitalist Ethos." *Legacy* 29.2 (2012): 201–21.

Wills, David. *Prosthesis*. Stanford: Stanford University Press, 1995.

Winship, Michael. *American Publishing in the Mid-Nineteenth Century: The Busi-*

ness of Ticknor and Fields. Cambridge: Cambridge University Press, 1995.

Wolstenholme, Susan. *Gothic (Re)Visions: Writing Women as Readers.* Albany: SUNY Press, 1993.

Wood, Marcus. *Blind Memory: Visual Representations of Slavery in England and America, 1780–1865.* New York: Routledge, 2000.

Index